# Beyond Regret:
# Living Victoriously in Christ
# After Abortion

**Written by:**
Sydna Massé

https://ramahinternational.org
https://herchoicetoheal.com
https://ramahsvoice.com

Ramah International

## Beyond Regret: Living Victoriously in Christ After Abortion

Published by Ramah's Voice,
Publishing arm of Ramah International, Inc.
Ramahinternational.org
HerChoicetoHeal.com
479-445-6070

# Beyond Regret: Living Victoriously

## Table of Contents

Introduction ...................................................................5

**Chapter 1 – Abortion's Ongoing Impact** ...............................**9**

Common Issues of Post-Abortive People ............................... 9

Abortion's Biological Impression .................................... 12

When Abortion is a Family Secret ................................... 19

How Abortion Can Impact Your Family ............................... 23

Fighting Forgetfulness ............................................ 26

**Chapter 2 – Ending Up in An Abortion Clinic** ....................**29**

Childhood Strife .................................................. 30

Survivor Guilt .................................................... 33

Abortion Decision Dynamics ........................................ 37

Previous Pregnancy Scares ......................................... 39

Abortion Influencers .............................................. 43

Teen Thought Patterns ............................................. 45

**Chapter 3 - Triggers and How to Tame Them** .....................**49**

You are Likely NOT Going Crazy! ................................... 49

Strategies to Tame Triggers of Abortion Pain ..................... 52

Exposure Healing .................................................. 59

**Chapter 4 – Demolishing Shame** .................................**63**

Removing Abortion Disgrace ........................................ 67

Why Didn't God Stop Me? ........................................... 69

**Chapter 5 - Good Grief** ........................................**73**

Fresh Grief ....................................................... 73

The Benefits of Grief ............................................. 77

Tears are Valuable to Your Health ................................. 78

**Chapter 6 - Overcoming Abortion Judgment** ......................**83**

The Murderer or Killer Label ...................................... 83

#ShoutYourAbortion Fallout ........................................ 86

Truth versus Condemnation...........................................................................91

Steps to Take When You Feel Abortion Judgement .......................................93

**Chapter 7 – Dynamics of Sharing the Secret ...................................97**

Four Costs of Sharing an Abortion Secret.....................................................97

What's Abortion, Mom? ............................................................................. 102

The Generational Cycle of Abortion............................................................ 105

Silent No More .......................................................................................... 106

Respecting an Abortion Secret ................................................................... 108

Don't Share Your Abortion Story with the Liberal Media ............................ 108

When You Shouldn't Share This Secret........................................................ 112

**Chapter 8 - Deeper Forgiveness ...................................................115**

God's Forgiveness After Abortion............................................................... 115

Forgiving Jane Roe: Abortion's Secondary Impact ...................................... 117

Stranger at the Abortion Clinic................................................................... 120

**Chapter 9 - Tackling Enduring Emotions ...................................127**

#MeToo and Abortion Pain ........................................................................ 127

Healing for Abortion's Ongoing Bloodguilt.................................................. 131

Addressing Abortion Clinic Verbal Abuse.................................................... 134

Five Types of Anger After Abortion............................................................. 137

**Chapter 10 – Thriving in Christ's Victory ...................................142**

You are Not Alone!..................................................................................... 142

How Many Women Have Chosen Abortion? ................................................. 144

God's Purpose in Abortion Pain ................................................................. 146

I Never Heard From Them Again................................................................. 149

## Introduction

*But you are a chosen generation, a royal priesthood, a holy nation, His own special people, that you may proclaim the praises of Him who called you out of darkness into His marvelous light…*1 Peter 2:9 NKJV

**Beyond Regret is a Bible study designed for those who have processed the emotions of grief after abortion through the *Her Choice to Heal* abortion recovery program.** This follow-up study builds on that healing by revealing issues that often impact the post-abortive life. It can be used after going through ANY abortion recovery program.

If you have not completed the *Her Choice to Heal* bible study, please realize that the initial grief work is the basis for the deeper healing with God. It is well worth the investment of your heart. Yet if touching that grief seems *too overwhelming*, **Beyond Regret** can be an easier place to begin your healing journey with God.

We all know that bible study programs do not heal a heart. They provide an outline on how to reach God who is the only healer of abortion pain. Accepting Jesus as your Savior is the first step.

The second step is to not only seek God within your heart and ask for His help, but also to have an ongoing relationship with the Holy Spirit until you reach your reunion with your child(ren) in heaven.

All you must do to receive the Love of Jesus is the following:

**Confess** that you are a sinner - Romans 3:23 *For all have sinned, and fall short of the glory of God.*

# Beyond Regret: Living Victoriously

**Recognize** that Jesus came and died for you even though you did not deserve it - Romans 5:8, *But God demonstrates His love toward us, in that, while we were still sinners, Christ died for us.*

**Admit** in your heart that Jesus is Lord, that He died for your sins, and rose again so that you could spend eternity in heaven with Him - Romans 10:9-10 -*That if you confess with your mouth the Lord Jesus and believe in your heart that God has raised Him from the dead, you will be saved. For with the heart one believes unto righteousness, and with the mouth confession is made unto salvation.*

Jesus wants to spend eternity with you. Even with your abortion sin, He still loves you and came to earth to die for you. He is crazy about you! Had you been the only person in the world - *and abortion your only sin* - God still would have sent His son to die for that sin.

God's initial healing after abortion provides significant peace once we forgive those involved in our abortion decision (including ourselves) and grieve the loss of our child(ren). There can also be a "let down" period where we can miss the fellowship and accountability that a group setting provided. There is also more work to be done in our hearts.

**Beyond Regret** has been developed to help you push deeper into the healing process with God. As someone who felt the peace that comes from completing an abortion recovery class, I know that God had more work to do in my heart in the months and years that followed. I am still a "work in progress." I can still stumble but God always is there to catch me.

Healing can also arrive in layers. When God rips away one layer, we find there are other zones that need to be addressed. These layers can be related to the abortion or other traumatic aspects of our past. The time I spent in God's word has allowed me to know God at a new level and receive the comfort of the Holy Spirit in my heart in a much deeper way.

God used the Holy Spirit to push thoughts into my mind when He wanted to get my attention. God speaks to us with our own voice in our heart. *Learning to understand His voice was the most important part of my healing journey.* As a result, the Holy Spirit has assisted me to overcome the common struggles of life after abortion victoriously, despite my past sins and shame.

Many of us did not know the feelings we would encounter after abortion. Now we have turned down a new road and we are unsure what to expect from our healing journey forward.

It is my hope that **Beyond Regret** will help you sort through these feelings and bring you closer to the tangible comfort of the Holy Spirit who can lead you through life with peace.

We know that the fellowship of other Christians can be a wonderful support throughout life. It is my hope that God will continue to touch your life with His healing and restoration.

### Comfort Scriptures

**Ecclesiastes 3:1-2, 4** - *There is a time for everything, and a season for every activity under heaven: a time to be born and a time to die, a time to plant and a time to uproot, a time to weep and a time to laugh, a time to mourn and a time to dance.*

**Psalm 37:23-24** - *If the LORD delights in a man's way, he makes his steps firm; though he stumble, he will not fall, for the LORD upholds him with his hand.*

## Activity

**Purchase** a plain paper journal to record your thoughts and complete the assignments listed after each chapter. You can record this information in a Word file or develop a video or audio file with this information.

**Commit** to reading one chapter in the Bible for 30 days. Begin with one chapter in John, Psalms or Proverbs. If you can read just one chapter a day for 30 days, your life will be completely changed!

# Chapter 1 – Abortion's Ongoing Impact

## Common Issues of Post-Abortive People

Post-abortion trauma has many "faces" depending on the variables surrounding the abortion situation and the fall out in our lives afterwards. The ordeal and time since making this choice, as well as ongoing healing in Christ, impacts ongoing peace as well.

This chapter is designed to educate about the common issues that impact a post-abortive life. Rarely does a post-abortive person suffer everything on this list. *Other symptoms may not even be included in the following list.* **This list reminds us that after the healing you can still encounter these issues.**

Because it is important to understand what emotions you may experience in the future, here are a few common issues that can present themselves during a post-abortive life experience:

**Guilt** – A mother's heart is genetically designed to, "protect her child at all costs." Abortion short-circuits that basic human genetic instinct. This can lead to feelings of guilt. A common guilty reaction after abortion could be that the person believes future bad events occur because they "deserve it" for choosing abortion.

**Anxiety (i.e., anxiety attacks)** - Many reveal that after their abortion they started feeling tense and could not relax. Some outline physical reactions like dizziness, pounding heart, upset stomach, headaches. They may worry about the future, struggle to concentrate and not be able to sleep. It is often difficult to understand the source of anxiety.

**Avoiding Children or Pregnant Women** – It is common for post-abortive people to avoid children, especially pregnant women or children that would have been around the age of their aborted child. This avoidance can include skipping baby showers, avoiding the baby aisle at the grocery store, walking around the block to avoid a playground, or making excuses to escape events that include children or pregnant women.

**Feeling "Numb"** – To avoid painful thoughts after abortion, many post-abortive people work to shut off their emotions. That could mean abandoning friendships and family, particularly if they remind them of the abortion experience. When someone shuts down emotionally, they do not feel sorrow or joy. Many turn to drugs or alcohol to assist in numbing these memories that result in guilt or anxiety.

**Depression** - Everyone is sad occasionally. After abortion, gloomy feelings can make the person feel hopeless and unlovable. They may cry uncontrollably for no reason and/or feel like they are going crazy. Perhaps they cannot eat or sleep or eat too much and sleep all day. The things they used to enjoy are avoided.

**Thoughts of suicide** – Some post-abortive people become so sad that they think it would be easier to die than continue living. Others miss their lost child so much that they want to join them to hold them at last.

**Anniversary Triggers** – This "anniversary" can be the aborted child's due date, or the date of the abortion. On these dates, the post-abortive can feel horrible for no apparent reason. It can take years to understand these dates are related to their abortion experience.

**Experiencing the Abortion Again** – A post-abortive person's mind can be suddenly transported back to the abortion clinic and re-experience their abortion. Memories can be triggered by simple sounds heard during the abortion procedure – like a vacuum cleaner or a dentist drill. For those who endured medical abortions, it can be the sound of a toilet flushing.

Yearly pap tests can also resurrect these memories. Others experience ongoing nightmares involving children, perhaps in pain. They can even have the same nightmare repeatedly.

**Wanting to get pregnant again** – It is normal to want to get pregnant again as soon as possible after *any* pregnancy loss. Most do so out of a desire to make sure they can still have a baby. Others hope to "replace" the life that was lost during the abortion. This is often referred to as an "atonement" or "replacement" pregnancy.

**Fear of Infertility** – Many women worry about being able to get pregnant again. They fear they have aborted the only child they will ever have. Others suspect the abortion could have mutilated their body in some way.

**Unable to Bond with Present or Future Children** – If the post-abortive person has children before or after the abortion, these family members can be a constant reminder of the person they aborted. This pain can result in the person distancing themselves emotionally or even abandoning these children, believing they are disqualified to be a parent.

**Fear that Their Children Will Die** – Some post-abortive people live in fear that children they had before or after the abortion could easily die. This fright can lead these parents to *overprotect* their children at an unhealthy level.

**Eating disorders** - Episodes of anorexia or bulimia is common for post-abortive people. Some get fat or thin to avoid anyone wanting them sexually as that could lead to another pregnancy. Eating is also something an individual can personally regulate when their life feels beyond their control.

**Alcohol and Drug Use** – Drugs and alcohol often serve as tranquilizers that help the post-abortive keep the memories of an abortion at a distance. They can help calm anxiety and promote sleep. Sadly, the overuse of these elements can lead to other problems at a mental and physical level.

### Abortion's Biological Impression

The biological impact of abortion is often the *least understood* aspect of this choice due to the lack of statistically significant scientific research. After abortion, women rarely reveal this truth to anyone. That fact alone makes research on the emotions after abortion *nearly impossible to verify*.

Even without detailed research on post-abortive experiences, science has provided proof of the biological impact of abortion. There are four ways in which a woman's body is physically impacted by abortion. As you review this information, I hope you will begin to understand some of the changes that happened to you due to your abortion.

**Hormonal Changes** - Every pregnancy involves giving birth when the child's placenta detaches from a woman's uterine lining. Abortion tears off that placenta artificially. When this happens, the woman's hormonal system is *shocked* to a certain extent.

It can take weeks to adjust back to pre-pregnancy stages. A positive pregnancy test can occur for four to eight weeks after abortion. This hormonal adjustment can result in **postpartum depression**, which can leave the post-abortive woman feeling overwhelmed, guilty, angry, or numb at the very least.

Many women reveal they feel "empty" after the abortion. The likely reason for this *empty* feeling is a result of the hormone, Oxytocin, streaming through a mother's body during pregnancy. *This hormone hard wires women to form enduring bonds with their children.*

# Beyond Regret: Living Victoriously

The minute a woman becomes pregnant, Oxytocin starts to flow, and the biological bonding process begins. Even when the tiny human is removed at the earliest stages of pregnancy, the mother still has that hormonal bond with her lost child.

Oxytocin makes memories vivid and long-lasting. Since these hormonal levels remain strong for several weeks after an abortion, abortion memories can be extremely vivid and graphic.

**Cellular Connection** - A study from the International Journal of Epidemiology reveals an incredible biological phenomenon known as **microchimerism** (https://pubmed.ncbi.nlm.nih.gov/16084184/).

*Simply explained, during the early stages of pregnancy, the mother and child exchange small quantities of cells. The ongoing cellular presence of this child in the mother's body is called microchimerism.* There is evidence that mothers are unconsciously influenced by fetal DNA for years after their pregnancies, if not for the rest of their lives.

This cellular connection was discovered when researchers found male DNA in a woman's bloodstream who had never given birth. In questioning this woman after the Y chromosomes were discovered in her blood, they learned she had aborted a child. These doctors then theorized that her aborted child must have been a boy and that some of his DNA remained in her body. *They concluded that cells of unborn children* **remain** *in the bodies of their mothers –* **whether they are aborted or brought to birth.**

Early in pregnancy, cells from the unborn child and it's mother travel across the placenta. This results in the two humans – mother and unborn child – *becoming part of each other.* Estimates suggest that as much as 10 percent of the mother's DNA in her bloodstream comes from the tiny human(s) in her womb. The child's DNA levels in the mother's body drops after birth but there is clear evidence that some remains.

In my post-abortive heart, the scientific concept of microchimerism explained why I could not forget the child I had lost in that abortion clinic. *My child was still part of me as his cells ran through my bloodstream.*

Post-abortive women often report feeling "haunted" at some point after abortion. Picture knowing something is wrong but being unable to define the situation.

When the aborted child's placenta physically detaches from her/his mother's womb, a difficult to explain *separation anxiety* can overwhelm the mother's heart. This "emptiness" often feels like a haunting as memories of the lost child surround the woman despite her never knowing this infant.

Everyone carries cells that were acquired from their biological mother. These cells continue to be present in our body when we become adults. Microchimerism is also prevalent in future pregnancies. Evidence shows that a mother's body retains a large amount of foreign material from each child that developed in her womb. This foreign material grows deeper and more complex in the mother's body over time.

This DNA can even be exchanged from older siblings to younger children, or across multiple generations. *The ongoing genetic material from lost children being transferred to the mother's future children explains why siblings who have brothers or sisters in heaven often feel a deep connection to their deceased family members.*

Personally, the cells of my two older sisters that died after birth due to separate birth defects are likely part of my own DNA today. This explains why I feel such a bond with these deceased sisters, *even though I never met them.* Their DNA runs through my body because my mother's body transferred them to me when I resided there.

This scientific concept of microchimerism also explained why my mother's heart could not forget my aborted child. We continue to maintain a biological connection at a cellular level. It also verified why I always felt so close to my own mother and my three sons as I was also cellularly connected to them.

Seven years after my abortion I gave birth again. When I looked in my newborn son's face, the presence of the child I had aborted came into my heart. The cellular and spiritual aspect of giving birth ignited the memory of the child I refused to acknowledge in my heart.

That haunting moment reminded me of Isaiah 49:16 – *Can a mother forget the baby at her breast and have no compassion on the child she has borne? Though she may forget, I will not forget you!*

During my abortion recovery class, I remember reading Jeremiah 31: 15-17 – *This is what the Lord says: A voice is heard in Ramah, mourning and great weeping, Rachel weeping for her children and refusing to be comforted, because they are no more." This is what the Lord says: "Restrain your voice from weeping and your eyes from tears, for your work will be rewarded," declares the Lord. "They will return from the land of the enemy. So there is hope for your descendants," declares the Lord. "Your children will return to their own land.*

This passage explains the microchimerism concept and the struggle to grieve children lost during pregnancy. The healing process involves *recognizing our aborted children as people.* We strongly encourage individuals to name their lost children and have a memorial service for them at the end of their abortion recovery process. If this is not possible, finding other ways to memorialize these children can be very healing. From designing a lovely piece of jewelry to planting a tree, God can lead you in this restorative endeavor.

During my own memorial service for my aborted child, whom I named Jesse, I went forward for prayer. The pastor asked for my child's name and proceeded to ask God to remove the grave clothes of this child from my heart. In that instant, I felt like I spiritually lost 40 pounds.

The Jeremiah 31:17 verse came into my heart as I sat down. My child had been welcomed into my heart, named, and grieved. In acknowledging Jesse as my own son, he returned from Satan's grasp to take his rightful place in my heart forever. Spiritually, Jesse returned from the land of the enemy and back into my heart. That brought great peace to my soul. Until I meet him in heaven, Jesse is safe in the arms of Jesus. His cells in my body keep him close to my heart until then.

**Your Grandmother Carried You!** - It is quite astounding to realize that we were all once part of our maternal grandmother's body. At around four months, eggs in a female fetus are created. Upon birth, a woman has all the eggs she will ever have in her lifetime.

When your grandmother was pregnant with your mother, you were a tiny egg in your mother's ovary. This is how your grandmother carried you. If you have a daughter, you carried your grandchildren in your body as well!

When I was seven years old, my family took a trip back to Ireland so my brother and I could meet our relatives there. While I was young, I vividly remember getting off the plane in Belfast, N. Ireland with the distinct feeling I was "home."

Everything seemed familiar to me, and I could not figure out why.

During that trip, my parents took me to visit my only living grandmother – my mother's mother. I was quite shocked to walk into her TINY row home which could not have been more than 900 square feet in size. Everything seemed familiar in that abode - *despite the fact I had never been there before.* This was the home where my mother had been born and raised.

Sadly, my grandmother physically abused my mother throughout her young life. Daily beatings focused on my mother's head were common. My mother would wake up at least monthly in the hospital after being knocked out cold. There were no laws in Belfast then relating to child abuse. No one intervened and my mother suffered horribly at the hands of my grandmother.

As I was walking around her home, I came downstairs to realize my parents had left me with this grandmother without saying goodbye. I was horrified that this woman could potentially beat me in that moment. She was not a person I wanted to stay with by any means. I truly did NOT like her at all!

She ignored my angst and quickly dragged me down the street to meet all her friends. I was introduced as "May's wee girl" and my cheeks were pinched hundreds of times it seemed. These Irish women would encourage me to speak and then laugh at my American accent. It was quite a difficult day in my young life – *the only one I would ever spend with this grandparent.*

During dinner back at her home, she prayed over the meal. Shocked that she spoke to God, I came right out and asked, *"Why did you beat my mother when she was a child?"*

Shocked at such an impertinent question from a seven-year-old, my grandmother simply denied my accusation saying in a serious tone, "I never laid a hand on your mother, Sydna." I did NOT believe her but asked no more questions since she was lying. My mother had shown me her scars and told me the stories of how her mother had inflicted each one. I wanted no part of such a brutal woman. I was not happy, and my body language and lack of words revealed that vividly. She did not seem to care.

When my father came alone to pick me up the next day, I was equally angry with him. In the car I blasted him with my anger over leaving me with this woman. He simply laughed and then told me to be quiet saying I should be thankful I had even met her.

My mother was later quite apologetic when I accused her of leaving me to be beaten in the same way she had. Her answer was, "Your grandmother clearly adored you so I knew you would be safe. She didn't care for your brother, however, so he stayed with us." I was jealous of my brother then, and he was angry at me because he wanted our grandmother's attention and did not receive it.

When I learned that I had literally RESIDED in my grandmother's body in egg form when she was pregnant with my mother, a deeper understanding took hold in my heart. I walked out that idea realizing that I had also been part of my mother's body during those horrifically abusive days. Each beating was something that impacted me too. How could it have not if I was inside her body at the time?

While research on how egg life can impact future generations who reside in their mother's bodies during abuse has yet to be completed, it isn't hard to draw conclusions. The horror of my mother's early abuse also impacted me at a biological level.

That led to another deeper understanding about one of my major reasons for aborting. I had made the choice to "protect" my mother from additional shame/guilt/grief of community rejection. I knew she would be deeply traumatized with a pregnant unmarried daughter. Hoping to spare her that shame, I embraced abortion for my own child, *who was once a part of my mother's body as well during my time in her womb!*

Take a few moments to remember your mother's upbringing and your relationship with your maternal grandmother. Trauma is typically repeated down the generational line. There is so much that we do not realize or understand because the truth of the past is rarely revealed.

Abortion has occurred in various forms for thousands of years. While you may never know what your ancestors experienced as it relates to an unexpected pregnancy, that doesn't mean their choices did not impact you eventually. Take a minute to ponder your maternal family history and connect any dots that may exist to your abortion experience.

**When Abortion is a Family Secret**

"My grandmother insisted I abort when I was 15," the woman shared. "She was an incredible person who raised me when my parents could not. I loved her completely. Sadly, when she discovered the father of my baby was 25 years older than me, her decision on my having an abortion was final. I had no choice in the matter."

# Beyond Regret: Living Victoriously

Few understand that women – *particularly minors* – may have **little choice** regarding an abortion because their families make the choice for them. In this woman's case, her child's father was a pedophile. For some sad reason, removing a pedophile's child from a young teenager's womb still seems appropriate, in even Christian families. Tragically, her abuser faced no charges and may have gone on to molest other teenagers. She was left spiritually broken by the abortion. It wounded her more than the pedophile's abuse.

No matter what the circumstances of conception, abortion can wound anyone at a spiritual, emotional, psychological, biological, and physical level. Denied a choice in whether their child will live or die, many go on to embrace other dysfunctional behaviors.

Over the years, many have shared with me their stories of having an abortion at their parent's insistence. These stories were varied. Perhaps the parents were in ministry, or they 2343 overwhelmed with health issues. Maybe they were older and do not feel they have enough time left to raise another child. Even more common, *they are more concerned with their family's reputation in the community if the child was conceived outside matrimony.*

When a child is conceived through sexual abuse, even pro-life hearts can insist upon abortion. There are millions of different ways an abortion can be coerced but the results are the same. *After abortion, one family member is dead while the other deeply wounded.*

When a woman herself makes this choice, it is normal for her to lay guilt on those who encouraged her to abort. Since she cannot divorce her family, her life can be miserable whenever she is around those that did not stop her from taking the life of her child. Holidays, weddings, funerals, and even causal dinners with this family often reignite the memories of her lost child.

Another woman shared, "My mother was angry when she dropped me off at the abortion clinic. I was crying, pleading for her to let me place the baby for adoption. She told me to, 'Shut up and get it done!' Afterwards, she insisted on taking me out shopping. My body felt broken, and walking was hard.

My mother's message over lunch was that I had experienced something that millions of women had chosen with no obvious negative impact. She said she would not let me cry over a 'blob of tissue' and told me to never mention my abortion to her again."

Being unable to express her emotions to her mother ensured that this woman endured an emotional separation. The young woman then turned to drugs and alcohol to cope with her sorrow. She searched for love and became pregnant again and would abort two more times without informing her mother.

Another common experience in families is eventually learning that abortion was chosen by their parents, grandparents and even great-grandparents. Sadly, *keeping abortion as a family secret often means that future generations may continue the same path as their ancestors and choose abortion*.

Even when the family is not involved in this choice, friends and family members RARELY want to talk about a past abortion. Many even discourage the abortion recovery concept by simply saying, "Why would you want to resurrect all that pain? It is in the past. Leave it there."

The problem is that the abortion is not in the past. It is often sheltered deep within the mother's heart, soul, and mind, constantly working to come to the surface by way of grief.

Dysfunctional behaviors that began with an abortion can then continue to impact future family members.

Eleven years after my own abortion, I felt led to attend an abortion recovery class. In sharing that idea with my husband, he relayed, "Why bring that up now? It's all in the past." I responded, "I'm not resurrecting that pain. *It is settled in my throat, and I cannot swallow it anymore.* I must find help."

By that time, I had two living children and could no longer escape the memories of my lost child. My husband understood that word picture and accepted my logic and wanted me to be more at peace. God had come to the end of the road with my heart and insisted that I drop my reservations and trust Him enough to attend an abortion recovery class.

My husband did not know the organization offering the abortion recovery program to trust them with my heart, especially at a spiritual level. He did not know if they were even Bible-based.

I was also not a "basket case" at that point. He thought I was stable and secure enough not to need extensive counseling that we simply could not afford. When he learned the abortion recovery class was free and Bible based, led by lay ministry leaders, he felt more at ease and agreed to support my healing journey.

Spouses and loved ones can rightfully be concerned that an abortion recovery class could wound loved ones further. They are *understandably protective.* My husband had one condition of my attendance – that I come home each night of class and share details with him of what God was doing in my heart. This made him part of my healing.

Before my recovery class, I never spoke about my abortion. It was a forbidden topic to my heart. My husband would later relay that he wondered how I could be so cold as to not miss my lost child. *It was not in my nature to be cold and not grieve this lost child.* In a way, my desire to address this pain came as a relief to him. It meant I really wasn't cold at all.

Participants in abortion decisions also impact the healing journey. These can include parents, friends or a partner/spouse who promoted the abortion as a good decision.

It is difficult to grieve around someone who shares guilt for a decision that caused so much devastation to our hearts. These abortion **enforcers** often discourage the person from healing because it could trigger their own guilt and shame.

Family secrets are crippling. When one family member finds God's peace, 2 Corinthians 4:2 becomes part of the entire family's healing – *Rather, we have renounced secret and shameful ways; we do not use deception, nor do we distort the word of God. On the contrary, by setting forth the truth plainly we commend ourselves to everyone's conscience in the sight of God.*

**How Abortion Can Impact Your Family**

Abortion impacts everyone, whether they know it or not. It is a choice that influences not only the woman but also everyone related to them.

When I decided to abort, I captured the false promise that my life would go on as if nothing happened. The choice seemed the best for everyone involved – particularly my family. I logically believed this choice would afford both myself, my present and future family several advantages:

- My parents would never be disappointed in discovering my loss of virginity
- Finishing college and having a fulfilling career would make my mother proud of me and support my future family
- I could still have children in the future

Leaving that abortion clinic, I was overwhelmed with unexpected emotions like guilt, shame, and anger. My body was also in deep physical shock from enduring the surgical procedure without anesthesia. My maternal hormones were thrown into disorder which also impacted my heart.

Many disturbing thoughts and fears overwhelmed me quickly, particularly that the abortion could impact my future fertility. I took control of those thoughts by telling myself – "I can't think about this now. I'll go crazy if I do." Drugs and alcohol helped me drown out those fears *for a while*.

I often drew upon anger to steel my heart against any emotional fallout from my abortion. As the days passed, my heart turned to stone. The fun-loving person I had been was replaced by a secretive and pained young woman. This new person impacted everyone I loved in many ways.

The impact of abortion on my life and family was as follows:

**Confusion** – Postpartum depression set in after my abortion as hormones still flooded my body. When I went home from college after my abortion, my parents noticed my personality change. Believing something was wrong, they pushed me for answers I refused to give. Never suspecting an abortion, they sadly adjusted to their obviously troubled daughter who bore no resemblance to the sweet girl who graduated high school the year before.

# Beyond Regret: Living Victoriously

**Anger** – I *blamed* my mother for my abortion even though she never knew I was pregnant. I reasoned if she had been emotionally available, I may have been able to turn to her with my pregnancy truth. My anger was directed at her for many years despite the fact she was innocent of all involvement. That was unfair, wrong, and typical. *I was able to avoid feeling guilty if I was blaming her.*

**Infertility** – When I attempted to get pregnant with my amazing husband's child, infertility hit our marriage. I never expected that I could have aborted my *only* child. *The idea that I could have done something as a teenager that would mean my husband may never hold his own child was overwhelming.* While my barrenness was medically remedied, many women may not be able to have children for a variety of reasons after abortion.

**Bonding** – Looking into the face of my newborn son, I experienced "*motherhood wonderment*" and immediately fell in love. My motherly love transitioned quickly into a horrific understanding, reminding me of the child I had lost to abortion. My aborted child then began to haunt my heart, impacting my ability to bond with my new son.

**Grief/Guilt** – While I do not know how she discovered my abortion secret, my mother confronted me about my abortion five years later. She then collapsed in grief for her lost grandchild. Her grief ushered a new guilt into my heart.

Thankfully, God healed all related family pain after my abortion recovery process. During the days before her death, my mother and I spoke often about heaven and those who would welcome her home. There was peace between us that can only come from God.

While my abortion clearly impacted my mothering ability until God restored my wounded soul, He eventually set everything right when I asked for His help.

My lost child was named and welcomed into my heart, so he no longer haunted me. My husband adopted this child in heaven as his own and our children know about their brother, Jesse, in heaven.

## Fighting Forgetfulness

"I know I had an abortion. I just can't remember any of the details," the woman shared with me through email. "My heart is broken that I could do such a thing and so easily forget it. Will I ever remember?"

After abortion, women typically work to forget they ever made such a choice. If pain and grief do not manifest themselves quickly, they can appear as a delayed reaction in years to come.

If pain medication was used in the abortion process, it can be difficult to remember all the unique details of such an event. Anesthesia provides temporary memory loss, making it difficult to recall specifics. Some women will forget they had anesthesia too!

When I entered the abortion clinic, I had the distinct impression that I would remember that day in detail for the rest of my life. My memory was always very brilliant, particularly during traumatic incidents.

After the brutal surgical procedure, my mind became deeply anxious. My boyfriend endured deep panic while waiting for me in his car. When I came out, he ran to me, picked me up off my feet and twirled me around saying, "Oh, Sydna. I thought they had killed you up there!"

In that moment, deep concern set in. I had never considered that a safe and legal abortion could have killed me. My next thought was, "*What other consequences could there be?*"

It was then that I stopped and purposely determined I would control my thinking to avoid any recollections of this memory. I was not going to think about it anymore. I would simply lock that memory in a special spot in my brain where access was denied.

My decision to forget was typical and normal among post-abortive people. Some can endure long periods of time without any recollection of their abortion experience. The psychological vault where this experience is stored can remain locked until a trigger of pain opens that door.

*Triggers are strong emotional reactions set off by something that reminds a person of the abortion event.* Music that was popular at the time of the abortion can activate memories unexpectedly. Meeting a child that would have been their aborted child's age can crack open their well-kept secret vault. Noises like a vacuum cleaner or a dentist drill can elicit panic quickly as they remind us of noises we heard in the clinic.

After a triggering event, *the abortion door opens in our heart.* Fragments of memories can present quickly. These thoughts are often scattered or jumbled initially, leaving the individual unable to push them back into their mental vault.

When that heart's door opens, it typically cannot be closed in the same way again. *All the energy that has been used to forget suddenly falters.* Then the recollections are impossible to stop, leaving the individual feeling like they are losing their minds.

God can bring these memories back into your heart. Many times, He will delay this process until you know His grace and mercy at a deeper level. While you may want all these answers now, give that desire back to God. He knows the future and the perfect moments when to reveal answers to your heart. You can trust Him on the timing of revealing everything you have forgotten in the past.

## Comfort Scriptures

**Isaiah 53:7** – *He was oppressed and He was afflicted, Yet He opened not His mouth; He was led as a lamb to the slaughter, And as a sheep before its shearers is silent, So He opened not His mouth.*

**John 8:32** – *Then you will know the truth, and the truth will set you free.*

## Activity

**Develop a timeline of that period of your life along with any other traumatic incidences.** Visit HerChoicetoHeal.com and go to Module 8. Then click the "Healing Activities" button and then Activity #1 - https://herchoicetoheal.com/wp-content/uploads/2019/10/timeline-activity-1.pdf.

This form provides you with directions on the timeline activity. Print it out and complete it for this chapter's activity. Then save it in a special place for additional memories that God may bring to your heart in the future. We will refer to this timeline in future chapters as well.

# Chapter 2 – Ending Up in An Abortion Clinic

Many do not realize how they were set up to abort in many ways. In the last chapter, we spoke about common issues and family dynamics as they relate to a past abortion decision. **The next step is to determine how you personally ended up in an abortion clinic.** The goal here is to not make the same mistakes again and to better understand the outside pressure that impacted your abortion choice.

A great deal of time is spent focusing on the devastation of an abortion decision in an abortion recovery program. That recovery process includes remembering and naming your lost child(ren). Once you have made this child a personal part of your heart by grieving his or her loss, other heart elements come to the surface.

The first element I addressed after my healing class was the general question – *"How did I end up in an abortion clinic?"* It was outside of my general character to have ever experienced abortion. How did I get there?

Old memories surrounded me from that time in my life, ignited by the abortion grieving process. I kept cycling through the same question - "How could I have done that to my own child?" I was my own worst enemy, despite all the healing from the class. Shame and low self-esteem surrounded me again. That came with an even more agonizing thought - *If I could choose something so horrible as abortion, what other poor decisions could I make in the future?*

Regardless of all the healthy steps I had taken with God towards forgiving the younger version of myself that made that choice, I would take two steps forward and then ten back. The shame and guilt continued to plague me.

**Little did I realize that God had only just begun my healing.** Each step in my walk with Him had to be realized deeply in my heart. Circumstances had to play out to help me understand God's plan for creating me. Maturity had to occur which could only come through life experiences. People had to pass away as well for God to bring me the answers I requested. It was not a quick process! *The result of the ongoing healing was a faith that can move mountains and incredible ministry success in serving God.*

Perhaps you are going through the same emotions and fears? This chapter will begin to pull the pieces of your life together to help reveal how you ended up in an abortion clinic(s).

### Childhood Strife

Family histories that include abortion often involve other traumatic events. Unplanned pregnancy often results after deep family strife as one generation significantly impacts another. *These strife cycles cascade down the family line often ending in a generational circle of discord.* Sadly, abortion decisions are often repeated down a family line.

A psychological test of the *impact of family strife on unplanned pregnancy* is entitled the "**Adverse Childhood Experiences (ACE)" test**. The ACE test breaks down family strife situations into eight experiences, including:

- Recurrent physical abuse
- Recurrent emotional abuse
- Contact sexual abuse
- An alcohol and/or drug abuser in the household
- An incarcerated household member
- Someone in the home who is chronically depressed, mentally ill, institutionalized, or suicidal

- Mother is treated violently
- One or no parents

A study in **Pediatrics** researched ACE results in comparison with teenage pregnancy - (https://pediatrics.aappublications.org/content/113/2/320) – revealed *that if your childhood experience included four or more of these variables, you were likely to have experienced an unplanned pregnancy.*

My abortion healing process required me to address my past family trauma. *It also helped me understand how the ordeals of my childhood led me into a teenage pregnancy which ended in abortion.*

When I personally took the ACE test, my score of 4 made the impact of my upbringing obvious. Here were some basic points about my early childhood strife:

- My parents often fought before separating which involved physical violence and ongoing emotional abuse – ACE score: 2

- Before their separation, my birthfather institutionalized my mother for several months to prevent her from filing for divorce which would have ended his career as a Baptist pastor – ACE score:1

- After their divorce, I was raised for a period by a single parent, having little or no contact with my birthfather – ACE score:1

One thing that was not included in this study were POSITIVE experiences in early life that **build buoyancy and impacted how the trauma affected a child**. It's easy to understand how a loving teacher, grandparent or friend can impact the cycle of strife in a family in a positive direction.

Despite my ACE score, my upbringing was not as horrible as others. My mother's best friend, *who took care of me while she was in a mental institution*, supported me emotionally and physically during that traumatic period of my life. She encouraged me that God had not forgotten me, and He would turn my family's turmoil into something that could be used for His good.

Several years later, my mother remarried a good man who . loved me deeply. Even though he did not share my faith in God, he was my hero and took care of us. He helped my mother's emotional well-being and provided for us financially. His love for us was fierce and we were spared the harsher realities of single parenting in the early 1970's.

When I was 21, I asked my stepfather if he would adopt me. He graciously agreed. When he was in the process of dying from lung cancer in 2007, he told the hospice medical teams that my mother and I "adopted" him! *My adoption was a real healing step in both our lives.*

Despite that bit of healing, my childhood strife would continue to haunt my heart, leading to dysfunctional decisions. When I went to college, I searched for a meaningful relationship. Sadly, a liaison with a fellow student involved more strife as alcoholism and sexual abuse were also involved.

This partner coerced me to abort which resulted in a violent and painful abortion experience. After that, I turned to drugs and alcohol to help combat my own spiritual, emotional, and psychological pain that resulted.

In taking the ACE test, *these childhood experiences were resurrected in my heart*. I could vividly see God's hand of protection over my young life. While my choices were not good ones, my early childhood trauma also included a salvation experience. God never left my side.

Joining an abortion recovery class was the first step in resolving my adverse childhood experiences by returning me to a personal relationship with God. Through Scripture and gentle leadership, I learned that God loved me despite any choice I made. The peace that passes all understanding took hold of my heart and I was able to forgive, not only myself, but my family members as well with God's help.

**Survivor Guilt**

"Sydna, I wouldn't change my life now," the young mother wrote. "I can't imagine life without my children today. If I had not chosen abortion, I may very well not have the kids I have today. That gives me immense guilt because I enjoy my life today."

Abortion finds many of us at a crossroads. Abortion decisions are often made under pressure by the father, friends or even family. Many feel immediate relief after abortion because their crisis has been resolved. That respite is often temporary, giving way often to deeper feelings of guilt and grief over time. Denial then arrives to help address the guilt with false mindsets that this "choice" had been a good one.

Denial requires a great deal of *emotional energy* to maintain and does not last forever. When denial breaks, the realization that a tiny human was lost in that choice can be difficult. Parents look at their living children and realize how their world would have been different had they not chosen abortion.

In these clear moments of understanding, *grieving an aborted child can seem like a betrayal to their living children*. Without choosing that abortion, children born since that choice likely would not exist.

God was clear about taking the lives of children He created, as revealed in Deuteronomy 30:19 – *This day I call the heavens and the earth as witnesses against you that I have set before you life and death, blessings and curses. Now choose life, so that you and your children may live.*

Many work to forget the added dysfunction they endured because they chose abortion. Rarely does abortion improve a life but often it leads to other problematic behaviors. Basic symptoms of abortion pain that we've already reviewed are typically part of the family dynamic after abortion.

Our lives would have been much different had we made another choice. Before healing, many are unable to fathom a life different from the one they are living and can feel quite guilty for being happy. That idea is quickly met with grief because to have this current life, *their child(ren) had to die.*

Keep in mind that God is the author of all life on earth. He knew the circumstances of our birth before He created us. Jeremiah 1:5 states – *Before I formed you in the womb I knew you, before you were born, I set you apart…*

This verse states that all our days were recorded in God's book before we were even conceived. God knew every child He created that would be aborted. He knew all about the rest of our lives – who we would marry, our children and how He would move to draw us closer to His grace and mercy.

Because of this Biblical truth, our lives today – *even with our choice of abortion* – is the one that God planned before the world was formed. While I miss my Jesse immensely and would love to go back and make another choice, that is not possible.

The siblings of aborted children can also struggle with a level of "survivor guilt" when they know about their aborted sibling. My oldest son was 13 years old when he commented, with a pained expression, *"I know losing Jesse was your biggest regret. But if Jesse had been born, I would not be here, Mom…."*

God helped me with a fast response as I could sense his survivor guilt since his older brother had to die for him to be alive. I responded, "That may be true, but God knew all about you before He formed the World. He knew that I would abort Jesse too and you can see by all that we do that God turned his death into something that has brought life to thousands of other children. So never believe that your life is wrong because Jesse's death was the only way you are living today. You know that we have turned Jesse's death into God's good **– and you are part of God's good**."

His smile in response calmed my heart as he realized he didn't need to have any survivor guilt.

This guilt is something I endured growing up as well, as I had two sisters in heaven. My mother endured three pregnancies before having a healthy child – a son, my brother. Since she wanted a daughter, she worked hard to get pregnant with me.

When we were doing a pregnancy center training seminar in the area where my sisters were buried, I went to visit their graves. It was the first time I had ever felt physically close to them. When I came home, I shared with my mother about that visit. I outlined how I had always dreamed of having my older sisters brushing my hair and keeping my older brother in his place.

My mother laughed and said, "Oh, Sydna, I never wanted four children. If just one of your sisters had lived, I never would have gotten pregnant with you..."

Survivor guilt hit my heart with her comment. I thought, "They had to die so I could be born." Thankfully, God helped me process that thought too.

As I pondered that reality, God reminded my heart of Jeremiah 1 again. He had my sisters safe in His care and was using me in a way that would certainly make them proud. There is no sin in heaven, so unhappiness does not exist there. God is the only judge.

This thought also brought unexpected comfort. I'm grateful that my two sisters were there to welcome home their nephew on that fateful day of his death.

Microchimerism impacted my love for these sisters too. Their cells were transferred into my body when my mother was pregnant with me. We had also all existed as eggs in our mother's womb. Siblings of aborted children, who were born **after** their mother's abortion experience, can feel this loss deeply as well on a cellular level. We will speak more about this in a later chapter.

The enemy enjoys plowing our hearts up with thoughts like these that are designed to increase our wounding and destroy our happiness. Abortion's lost children are safe and at peace in the company of their Creator. Until the day comes when we meet them, God wants us to find His healing so that we can live life in peace and be used by Him in various ways to reach others.

## Abortion Decision Dynamics

Now that you realize that your childhood experiences impacted your arrival at an abortion clinic(s), it is time to go the next step to consider what impacted your vulnerability to abortion. *The more you learn about how/why women chose abortion, the more your own situation will make more sense in your heart.* This level of understanding was priceless in my life and walk with God!

While we have gone through the direct family impact with the ACE test, let's review more background elements that influence most abortion decisions. I compiled this list after listening to tens of thousands of abortion testimonies. *As you read through this list, highlight any that relate to your life*:

**Divorce** – A parent's divorce or trouble with a spouse can greatly impact a person's level of love. This leads to a search to replace the love that was lost. Often stepparents enter the house and assume leadership. Depending on the compassion of the stepparent, the child can still have a difficult time in losing their parent from their daily lives.

**Sexual abuse** – This includes incest, molestation, rape, fondling, etc. When someone has been subjected to perversion, and their virginity lost or compromised, they often feel led to continue in promiscuity believing the sexual act is "true" love. These individuals can have a twisted perspective of love, and some cannot relate to the word or emotion. They OFTEN experience abortion as a result.

**Death** – Sometimes the death of a close friend or family relative can leave a person vulnerable and alone. A loving grandmother's death can end in unexpected emotional turmoil, leading them to searching for love through sexual activity. These hearts are searching for comfort and simply believe sex can provide that consolation.

**Torment** – Bullying and teasing by peers or siblings can result in tremendous terror and loss of control that can easily lead to promiscuity and abortion. Most are simply searching for acceptance and love. If this bullied person becomes pregnant, they are then terrified of the taunting that could result. With no one supporting them, they typically choose abortion.

**Self-esteem** – Low self-esteem can lead to the desperation of searching for love in all the wrong places! This often begins at birth when parents are less than positive about their children's accomplishments and dreams. It is easy to be pushed into doing things they may not want to do.

**Parent's abortion** – An unhealed post-abortive parent may be unable to bond with their children. That can lead them to be overprotective and even threatening resulting in a dysfunctional home. If their child becomes pregnant, abortion is the only choice offered. "It worked for me, and it will work for you" is often the mindset.

**Cultural aspects** – In some cultures, virginity is critical. Should it be discovered that a woman has lost her virginity, she can be put to death because she has brought dishonor to her family. Abortion is the only way to spare this woman a death sentence.

**Trauma** – Physical abuse - *especially from boyfriends or husbands* - can easily lead a person to consider abortion in the incorrect conclusion that abortion would *protect* the child from harm. Very few realize that abortion is the ultimate form of child abuse.

**Media influence** –Abortion is sold as a cheap eraser should a *mistake* happen after sex. Rarely do women even hear about the suffering and pain of abortion expressed through these channels.

**Physical impairment** – Individuals who are physically handicapped (i.e., deaf, blind, lame, etc.) can often view themselves as incapable of parenting. This means abortion is their only choice if they become pregnant.

Did any of these elements impact your abortion decision? If so, write them down and take time to pray over them.

## Previous Pregnancy Scares

"My pregnancy test was negative, Sydna," the teenager texted me. "I'm so glad that we talked about how abortion impacts women and I got to hear about your abortion experience. I cannot believe abortion was even something I even considered. I have now made a vow of secondary virginity. I will never put myself in that position again."

Abortion is completely hypothetical until you find yourself looking at a positive pregnancy test. A pregnancy scare can lead anyone to consider the abortion option. However, when those individuals who considered themselves "pro-life" abort, their pain afterwards can be greatly intensified because they clearly "knew better."

When a period is late, *abortion is commonly the first thought*. After all, abortion is supposedly a safe and legal choice in America, even if you consider it to be murder. Without abortion's ability to eliminate a "problem" should one be conceived, many would not be having sex outside of marriage.

With a negative pregnancy test, many may later feel guilt for considering abortion, even if they did not choose it. When you stare into the face of a newborn that was conceived unexpectedly – *where abortion had been considered but not chosen* – regret and guilt can still result.

When I was considering abortion, my church had been silent on abortion. I never knew anyone protesting this choice or heard a pastor preach against it. I became sexually active right out of high school. I quickly ended up in an abortion clinic. If I found myself in such a horrible place, *anyone can*.

My abortion decision was DEEPLY influenced by two previous **pregnancy scares**. The first occurred after I lost my virginity. Waiting for my period to arrive then was a nightmare. I was starting college in two months. When I proposed abortion, my boyfriend insisted that we would be "forced" to marry because abortion was "wrong."

I didn't know why abortion was wrong, but I certainly did not want him to feel forced into marrying me! He obviously winced as he shared this truth, revealing marrying me was not what he wanted either. My heart grew hard towards him then because he offered me no comfort.

I soon vowed to never see him again. If I was pregnant, I determined to lie to him and have an abortion. He would never discover the truth. *Many men have no idea their children were conceived, let alone aborted.* When my period arrived on schedule, sweet release flooded my soul.

The second pregnancy scare occurred while I was out of the country on a college trip six months later. Since my virginity was gone, there seemed no good reason not to be sexually active. My period was ten days late when I returned home.

During those agonizing days, I searched for information on abortion. I am confident that I would have aborted then had I been pregnant. When my period arrived, I became firmly pro-choice.

Soon after that second pregnancy scare, I met my aborted baby's father. He insisted upon a sexual relationship. Since I was not a virgin, I agreed but hated that part of our relationship. There was no pleasure for me. When I got pregnant that summer, abortion was the only option he would support.

He threatened that if I did not abort, he would tell everyone it was not his child and leave me. After two pregnancy scares – *with abortion being the chosen solution* – I agreed to his demands.

He took me to a Planned Parenthood office for my pregnancy test. It was there that the final decision was made. No other support was offered other than abortion. At 19 years of age, abortion seemed like the *only logical* choice. I was sadly mistaken. It was the worst thing I had ever done in my life.

Years later – *after God did a miraculous work in my heart to help relieve me of the burden of those sins* – I could see how my eventual abortion decision took root the night I lost my virginity. Slowly but surely, with God's help, I began to understand how that first sinful step had led me into an abortion clinic where the tiny human in my womb died.

Had I visited a pregnancy center versus Planned Parenthood, I believe my child would be alive today. Pregnancy centers offer complimentary and essential pregnancy services and accurate abortion procedure information. These non-profit centers also provide physical and emotional assistance as well. The ministry services of pregnancy centers are essential for a woman to have a real choice for her pregnancy.

If not pregnant, pregnancy center clients typically rethink their abortion ideology due to the truth they received at the pregnancy center. A first pregnancy scare can then end any abortion consideration in the future. Women are empowered to make better choices. Many simply stop having sex outside of marriage then.

On the other hand, if women visit a Planned Parenthood, basic information about abortion is often ignored or discounted. I never knew abortion could impact me emotionally and psychologically. Rarely are physical and emotional support offered at organizations that sell abortions.

The consequences of a true pro-life heart choosing abortion is quite different than making this choice without knowing any better. Those that should know better than to have sex outside of marriage can be even more susceptible to choosing abortion should a pregnancy result.

Those that battle to save tiny humans at a legislative level typically have a different heart than those offering ministry services directly to abortion-vulnerable people in pregnancy centers. Fighting to end abortion politically is quite different from helping stop abortion one life at a time in ministry situation. Pro-life does not mean sin free or even "Christian."

Always remember that there is no sin that God cannot forgive and heal! You just may not forgive yourself and need a little help. By praying this verse, God can help begin your restoration – Psalm 139:24 – *See if there is any offensive way in me and lead me in the way everlasting.*

Take a moment to think through the day you lost your virginity and how it may have impacted your abortion decision. Record these thoughts and pray through them, asking God to help you understand your mindset in those years.

**Abortion Influencers**

The next step in understanding how you ended up in an abortion clinic is to consider those who influenced this decision. Identifying those who directly impacted your choice should have been part of your initial abortion recovery healing class. Now it's time to realize how others may have impacted your choice.

When an unplanned pregnancy is possible, a woman normally *endures a state of intense self-analysis*. Until she has her period, she will act under the mindset of, "What if I am pregnant?"

In this spot, a woman often turns to others for insight. These individuals then walk through the stress of the unplanned pregnancy until either the menstruation cycle begins, or the pregnancy test is positive.

The normal range for this crisis is 5-30 days. The source of information becomes an *influencer to the abortion decision*. They normally fall into five categories, which are impacted by the woman's level of self-esteem and age:

**Sexual partner(s)** – Normally, the key influencer of an abortion decision is the sexual partner. If the potential pregnancy is a result from a "one-night stand" or a "date/rape" situation, this influencer has a minimal impact on the abortion decision. It could also be that the child's father is unknown based on multiple sexual encounters. In that situation, the sexual partners can have little influence.

If there is a relationship in place with the sexual partner, *he becomes the key to the abortion choice*. The impact of this influencer depends on the perspectives of other involved individuals.

**Woman's Parents** - The woman's parents are normally the second strongest influencer after the sexual partner. More women are afraid of telling their parents they are no longer virgins than of relaying they are pregnant. The parents may never even know about the pregnancy but can still influence the decision. Many respond, "My parents will kill me if they find out I am pregnant."

**Man's Parents** - The sexual partner's parents also can play a pivotal influence role. Many are protective of their son's financial liability in a woman's pregnancy. They can doubt their son's parentage of the child and actively work to remove him from the woman's life by facilitating her abortion.

We have all heard the stories of these parents, primarily mothers of sons, who speak directly to the young woman to promote the abortion option. These parents can actively promote a life decision as well with offers of housing and support. Their love can certainly make the difference in her choice.

**Siblings** – Siblings of the man or woman involved in the unexpected pregnancy are also key influencers. Previous pregnancies with siblings can either encourage or discourage an abortion choice.

For example, consider the situation where the previous sibling placed her child for adoption. This individual will have firsthand experience about the emotional trauma involved in both pregnancy and adoption. Her perception is often that her parents will probably "make" her choose adoption and abortion may seem like a much more desirable choice. Still other siblings who are post-abortive may also influence an abortion decision to prove that their choice was the best.

**Friends** – While normally the least equipped to help, friends of both the man and woman can be strong influencers in the abortion decision. While the man may initially be supportive of a birth choice, his friends may "call him out" for such a stance and he can feel the pressure of these peers to reverse his initial reaction to the pregnancy. Women who have chosen abortion often encourage abortion among their friends as well.

Horror stories of struggling teenage parents may place a great deal of fear in these hearts as well. The best friends are those who lead their friends to a pregnancy center for support and information.

**Faith Background** - More Christians find their way into abortion clinics than those who express no religious background. This is because many are afraid to be honest with their "church" about their pregnancy or bring shame onto their family.

Abortion is then viewed as a logical choice as it can "erase" the mistake and allow them to go on with their lives without anyone knowing their "sin." If the person really believes in God, they may be asking Him to supernaturally stop them from aborting or give them a sign of what to do.

**Teen Thought Patterns**

Teenage brains are not fully developed until they reach 25 years. If a woman has an unexpected pregnancy as a teenager, she views the world differently from an adult. If you experienced abortion as a teenager, be aware of the following three common mindsets of this age group as it was likely part of your abortion decision-making process.

**Sense of permanence** –Teens tend to believe that how they feel today, as well as their current circumstances, are permanent. They believe that things will not change. No matter what you say or do, you cannot change their minds. They just do not seem to grasp that tomorrow their circumstances will be completely different and that their feelings/perspectives will not be the same.

In a similar sense, they believe that their relationships will always be as they are now. Their connections with their parents will always be "as is" and that their boyfriends will always feel the same way. Their friends will be their friends forever. The clubs and groups they belong to are going to still be the most important thing in their lives in ten years. They simply cannot comprehend that life is not that permanent.

**False knowledge of options** -- Teenagers have an "ideal" about their future. They grow up in schools that promote independence. When it comes to pregnancy, they are told repeatedly of the trials and ordeals of "struggling single moms." They often hear stories from the point of view of these women's children who have experienced "hardships" without a father.

They are rarely told of the awesome triumph of these women, and the wonderful things they accomplish. Schools can push children to understand the hardships of other people's lives to instill "tolerance." However, in doing so, it instills fear.

No woman wishes a hard life on her child, and the fear of what "could" happen often overtakes her. It is hard to "undo" the years of indoctrination that is imposed upon her by her teachers, parents, and culture. It is hard for her to understand that the people that she trusts do not know everything. She cannot believe that she can go on to finish high school, or college, or have a career if she continues the pregnancy.

**Invincibility belief** -- Teenagers often believe that they are immune to anything that is not within their scope of comprehension. When they find themselves pregnant, it seems "unreal" to them. While you may be able to explain the possible outcomes and complications, or future ramifications of an abortion decision to an adult, the teenager does not believe that any of that could ever pertain to them.

When you tell a teenager that she could suffer great emotional pain, she can raise an eyebrow and wonder if you honestly think she is crazy. If you tell her that she may never be able to conceive again, not only is that some "abstract possibility" to her, but she may also believe you are an "alarmist" and are using "scare tactics."

I hope that this discussion has given you some insight into where you were emotionally, spiritually, and psychologically when you made the decision to have an abortion. I encourage you to prayerfully ponder your own life and how the information in this chapter could have impacted your choice.

## Comfort Scriptures

**Psalm 40:1-3** – *I waited patiently for the Lord; he turned to me and heard my cry. He lifted me out of the slimy pit, out of the mud and mire; he set my feet on a rock and gave me a firm place to stand. He put a new song in my mouth, a hymn of praise to our God.*

**1 Peter 2:24** – *"He himself (Jesus) bore our sins" in his body on the cross, so that we might die to sins and live for righteousness; "by his wounds you have been healed."*

## Activity

**Complete the ACE Test** - You can find one at this link - https://www.npr.org/sections/health-shots/2015/03/02/387007941/take-the-ace-quiz-and-learn-what-it-does-and-doesnt-mean.

Pray and ask God to reveal the situations that impacted you in the days of your abortion. Consider each situation of trauma and record as much as you remember of those situations in your journal.

Make a list of those individuals that helped during those moments of trauma. Consider the positive influence of outsiders in your life during those days. Remind yourself that God often uses humans to be His hands and feet in helping us.

**Ponder how others influenced your abortion decision.** This chapter shared more about the dynamics of an abortion decision, mindsets that impact abortion decisions, abortion influencers and teenage thinking patterns. *Did any of these points hit home in your experience?*

If so, take time to go through each memory. Then record this part of your life (i.e., video, writing in your journal, audio, etc.) and review it with God. Ask God to help you visualize His being with you along each step of your life journey.

## Chapter 3 - Triggers and How to Tame Them

With Abortion PTSD trauma, it is normal for sights, sounds, smells and even feelings encountered during the time of the abortion to ignite memories you have been working to forget. These **triggers** can then initiate emotional, psychological, spiritual, and physical reactions, bringing the abortion pain to the surface of our heart.

*It is important to understand why we react in certain ways and recognize what has set us off.* This chapter is designed to help you determine what elements in your future life could "trigger" this past abortion pain. Then, when such a trigger arrives, you can then understand it and work to tame it so that it does not have the same impact on your heart in the future.

### You are Likely NOT Going Crazy!

The first thing to realize is that when you react in an unexpected way to something, you are not going crazy. This is a common myth of post-abortive people when their reactions are quite normal.

One day I found myself sitting waiting for a new dentist. My healing was well in place. I had been teaching about abortion triggers and taming them for years. This office had an open floor plan. I could see the dentist working on the person two chairs down. I also heard all the sounds of the dental equipment as I waited for nearly thirty minutes.

Oddly enough, I grew incredibly angry. My upset seemed outlandish, but it wasn't going to be denied. I felt I had to get out of that office, or I would lose my mind! God helped me calm myself, take a few breaths and analyze my situation.

Instantly I remembered that the sound of a dentist drill often triggers my memory of the sound of the abortion suction machine. With that clarity, I felt deep relief in realizing why I had grown so upset. I had forgotten all about my issues with sounds, particularly in a dentist's office. I had walked in *without* my taming headsets that could block this noise with music.

With that realization, *I knew it was okay to be upset.* I also realized I needed another dentist with a different floorplan! I still got my teeth cleaned that day but never returned. Each time I make a dental appointment, I make a note to have my trigger taming plan in place. In other words, I have a way to block the triggering sound of that dental drill!

No matter how healthy you are or how close you are to Jesus, you can experience triggers and unexpected reactions. While discussed previously in this book, common triggers of post-abortion pain include, but are not limited to:

**Media Mention** – Abortion is an ongoing hotly debated political topic that is discussed often in media channels. Every time the word "abortion" is overheard, the pain within the heart of the post-abortive individual can be triggered.

**Sounds** – Noises that resemble those overheard during the abortion time frame can trigger Abortion PTSD pain. Music that you enjoyed during that period in your life can remind you of this choice. Vacuum cleaners and dentist's drilling noises can leave post-abortive women in deep anxiety as they remind us of the abortion suction sound. For those who endured medication abortion, the swish of a toilet flushing can produce pain and trauma, particularly if they flushed their aborted children after they passed from their bodies.

**Anniversary Dates** – The due date of the aborted child or the anniversary of the abortion experience often finds post-abortive individuals battling bouts of depression. When individuals work to forget their abortion, these dates are often difficult to recall. It can take years for the person to identify these dates as events of anxiety and pain in their lives.

**Pregnant Women and Young Children** – In the months following an abortion, pregnant women who have a similar due date as the post-abortive woman can be powerful reminder of loss. After their aborted child's due date has passed, encountering children that are the same age of their lost child can also ignite anxiety.

**Intimacy** – Sex is a reminder of how we got pregnant in the first place so it can be a powerful activator of post-abortion pain. If the woman is unmarried, each sexual encounter could produce another unexpected pregnancy that may require another abortion. For married women, husbands often have no idea an abortion has taken place and suffer in sexless marriages. After abortion pain can also ignite sexual promiscuity, leading to many dysfunctional related behaviors like drug/alcohol abuse, eating disorders, etc.

**Motherhood Moments** – It is difficult to investigate the face of a newborn and experience motherhood wonderment and not be reminded of the child you aborted. If the woman was a mother at the time of her abortion, looking into her living children's faces can prompt memories of their child lost to abortion. Milestone marks that would have been reached had the child lived – like graduation from kindergarten, high school, or college – can also remind the woman of her child in heaven.

**OB/GYN Check-Ups** – One thing I never expected after my abortion was how difficult it would be to be honest about this procedure on a routine doctor's intake form. I felt a deep fear each time I encountered one of the most difficult medical questions for a post-abortive woman – number of pregnancies.

**Political Debates on Abortion** – When politicians outline their views on abortion and detail their plans to either enhance or diminish abortion rights, anxiety is often produced in post-abortive listener's hearts. Many have no idea that in many areas, abortion is legal up until a child's delivery date. Hearing someone defend abortion can also ignite this pain and trigger deep anger.

Thankfully, there can be positive fallout from this ignited pain. At some point, many can no longer cope with ongoing triggers and seek out help by turning to God. Jesus Christ died on the cross for every sin – even abortion. By believing in Him, we are set free from this emotional prison and allowed to live a life free of condemnation and shame.

**Strategies to Tame Triggers of Abortion Pain**

"It's my baby's due date next week, Sydna," the writer outlined. "How do I cope with this reminder each and every year for the rest of my life?"

My first abortion trigger came seven months after my abortion – *on my child's due date*. I never connected the horrendous evening I spent locked in a dorm room crying as the night I should have been giving birth to my child. I thought I was losing my mind as there was no obvious reason for such an intense emotional reaction. I refused to think about my abortion so that wasn't even considered.

The next morning my eyes were swollen shut from crying. I went to the campus health center in a deeply demoralized state and discovered I did not have pink eye. It was clear that my poignant pain was odd. For many months I felt like I was on the verge of insanity.

When I read about Abortion PTSD eleven years later, I was relieved to discover the reason for my emotional angst back then. I could look back on the last eleven years of agony surrounding the third week in March when my child should have been celebrating a birthday. Once I realized this date was a trigger to my pain, I was able to tame that trigger and plan ways to cope.

Here are some methods to tame triggers of Abortion PTSD:

**Document your trigger dates on a calendar**– If you have had more than one abortion, or don't remember exact dates, don't worry. Record dates when you felt depression or experienced pain that seemed to have no source.

**Develop distraction strategies**– As I said previously, for every dental visit, I now arrive at these appointments with a headset to listen to music to offset any triggering noises. If I suddenly feel upset while vacuuming, I stop and pray, asking God to help me in this task.

**Participate in positive life-affirming activities**– Writing a tax-deductible donation check and/or helping at a pregnancy center can aid your tender heart. Encouraging those continuing an unexpected pregnancy with thoughtful gifts or lunch can also be beneficial.

**Sooth your heart with Scripture** – The Bible is filled with redemptive stories of sinners that help teach God's forgiving nature. David's unexpected pregnancy with Bathsheba, found in 2 Samuel 11-12:25, outlines we are not alone in the taking of an innocent life. David walked with God at the time he had

Bathsheba's husband murdered. God sent Nathan to help show David his sin. After David repented, God gave him another son – Solomon – who would succeed him as King of Israel. Reviewing the stories of Adam and Eve eating the apple and the Apostle Paul can also help.

**Control your anger**– Becoming irritable upon hearing individuals promote abortion as "safe and legal" can trigger Abortion PTSD rage quickly. While the abortion outrage can appear like "righteous indignation," we can certainly sin in our responses. Deep seated anger can result as our abortion wound erupts. Remember to emanate Godly behavior, as outlined in Psalm 86:15, *But you, Lord, are a compassionate and gracious God, slow to anger, abounding in love and faithfulness.* Take a "time out" to gain control of your anger.

**Writing out your story**– Recording the story of your life can help you realize what made you susceptible to an unexpected pregnancy and abortion. That can provide perspective that God can use in the healing process. Begin with the story of your family and include a full account of what led you to lose your virginity. List out your fears at that time. For example, "I feared my mother more than God. I wanted to believe the lies." Then document the dates of deep pain.

**Pray to seek God's help directly**– The Creator of the Universe offers the best comfort. Seek Him with an open heart and a sincere, "Help me, God" prayer. Acts 17:27-28 outlines, *God did this so that they would seek him and perhaps reach out for him and find him, though he is not far from any one of us. 'For in him we live and move and have our being.'*

**Discover Supportive Friends** – Ramah International exists to help connect abortion's wounded heart to their local abortion recovery team for direct ministry. If you have not completed an abortion recovery program, please prayerfully consider one. Understand that many emotions can become stronger when they are ignored.

**Keep track of your anniversary dates and make plans for those dates -** Try to plan something on these dates to occupy your mind or to specifically remember your child in heaven. Ask friends to pray for you during this time, that God would continue to comfort your heart.

**Secure Prayer Coverage -** If you know of an unhealed abortion wound, or are facing hostile or involved family members, be sure to ask for prayer coverage before any family event. If confrontations could be looming during the family gathering, it's best to have God involved.

**Initiate New Family Traditions -** For those who may have encouraged or discouraged the abortion, they also need God's grace and mercy evident during the meal versus tension and discord. Starting a new tradition of having a moment of silence to memorialize family members who have passed away is a great idea. Using this time to allow yourself to memorialize the aborted child can be very healing. Understanding that this child is in God's good care can be comforting as well.

**Holiday Events** - Holidays are a fact of life. Gathering with people who could have encouraged or discouraged a choice to abort often activates old memories of abortion pain. While many will avoid these gatherings, others do not have that luxury.

For those that have not embraced God's healing after abortion, family meals can be a traumatic experience. Consider eating turkey while sitting next to the aunt who dragged you off to the abortion clinic? Or with the cousin who previously bragged about her two abortions?

An abortion decision is often wrapped in deep emotions with multiple people offering their advice or family members who force an abortion decision. Rarely is the abortion ever discussed afterwards.

Sharing a meal with someone who was involved in an abortion decision can ignite anxiety along with other emotions like shame, hatred, and disgust. The undercurrent of such a meal is often uncomfortable. Obvious grief often goes unrecognized as most around the table do not even know an abortion occurred. If they do know about it, they are unaware of the pain the woman is enduring.

Many women also can face hostility from those who worked to discourage their abortion decision. Underlying emotions of anger and hatred can still rage in these hearts against the post-abortive person making it difficult to even converse. Unforgiveness and grief often make these relationships impossible.

Having a meal with those who recommended abortion can also trigger difficult memories. While the abortion may never be mentioned, that does not mean the abortion wound is not inflamed.

Few of us realized when we chose abortion that reminders of our lost child would surround us as we grew older. Seeing a person even today that is the same age as Jesse would have been, can impact me. I never thought I'd be grieving the potential grandchildren Jesse would have provided to my life.

Whenever these triggering events arrive, it makes no difference. *A past abortion can be suddenly illuminated in the secret room of a person's heart and the light may never go off again until God restores them to His peace.*

Thankfully, there is the hope of God, whose desire is to heal this part of our hearts. His grace and mercy can bring us to the point where we can forgive ourselves for making such a choice – or offer mercy and forgiveness to those who aborted a loved one – grieve this lost child and find joy again.

**Specific Christmas Pain** - "My child would have been born by now and enjoying Christmas," a recently post-abortive women shared. "Will Christmas always remind me of the child I aborted?"

During Christmas, many discover that their emotional and spiritual pain related to this choice can peak, robbing them of any seasonal joy. My husband and I celebrated Christmas with full hearts in 1988 because of the gift of our newborn child. One night before Christmas Day arrived, I awoke to the sound of a baby crying. As I rose to tend to my infant, I realized my son was fast asleep in his bassinet beside my bed.

When the child's cry sounded again, I got up and went through my house and noticed our beautiful Christmas tree. A familiar emotion crept into my heart. *A child was missing from our celebration – the one I had aborted as a teenager.* As I heard the unknown child's cry again, I attempted and failed to put the thought of my lost child out of my heart.

I found the sound was coming from our baby monitor. It was picking up the transmission of another unit nearby. I then heard that child's mother coming to provide comfort.

The experience of that sound in my house ignited my abortion grief. I could not stop the sobs that then overwhelmed me as I realized my child's death again. In realizing all the Christmas moments I had missed with my aborted child, my soul was filled with deep regret.

**Embrace the Tears -** Psalm 126:5 reveals that tears lead to joy – *Those who sow with tears will reap with songs of joy.* Fearful of a mental breakdown, post-abortive hearts often believe that if they start crying, they won't be able to stop. Yet tears are the body's way of ridding itself of toxins which makes grieving good for our health.

Humans never get over grief. We simply get through it. When my parents passed away, I learned this truth at a deeper level. I never want to "get over" their deaths. They will remain precious people in my life, and I will miss them forever. Anniversary dates of their death, birthdays and tangible items continue to remind me and comfort me in living on Earth without them.

It is the same in my heart when I grieve my child. Tears are precious to God. As the Psalm 125:5 verse listed previously reveals, weeping draws us closer to God's everlasting arms. By embracing grief, we can discover His peace and comfort.

God can release the guilt of the loss of these precious children. Tears begin God's cleansing process, starting the process of settling His peace in your heart. Please allow yourself to mourn. Grieving a child lost to abortion typically helps calm abortion pain at a temporary level. Allow the poison to be washed away with your tears.

Weeping also begins God's cleansing process, starting the settling of His peace into your heart to help you cope and endure. Crying releases deep emotions and lifts burdens, bringing God close. Don't be afraid of tears but embrace them!

**Develop Tangible Reminders -** Because there is no graveside to visit after a child dies from abortion, most post-abortive people have no place to go to grieve. Society often outlines that if you made this choice, you don't deserve any comfort. Few ever have a funeral or memorial service for their aborted child unless they participate in the abortion recovery process.

Memorials don't need to be extensive. Some have planted a tree in their back yard to remind them of the child they lost to abortion. Others create beautiful works of art or purchase "mother's rings" with a gemstone that matches their child's potential due date.

Christmas is another season where tangible items can be a comfort in future years when the memories of these lost children are triggered. One woman shared, "Last year I bought a beautiful crystal ornament as a memorial to my child. This year it doesn't hurt me to look at it and put it on our tree. In fact, it is a real comfort!"

**Exposure Healing**

Over the years, I have purposefully walked through many locations that housed disturbing memories. "Exposure therapy" is a clinical term for this process of ending any avoidance of PTSD triggers that might remain or even intensify over time.

Early in my ministry life, I felt God urging me to visit places that held traumatic memories. One locale was the college that I attended at the time of my abortion. When a director from a pregnancy center near that college invited me to speak at their banquet, it was clearly God's time to revisit that campus.

As those arrangements were made, I felt relief that I would only be walking around the campus and not actually sharing my testimony to the student body. Several days later, after concluding a Focus on the Family broadcast taping in 1996,

Dr. James Dobson asked a simple question, "How are you doing, Sydna?"

I responded without thought, "I'm going back to Taylor University to walk through those memories."

Dr. Dobson responded, "You are going to speak when you are there, right, Sydna?"

"No," I responded. "I don't know how one invites themselves to speak there. I just want to put those memories to rest by walking through them."

Dr. Dobson smiled and said, "I will personally take care of that speaking invitation, Sydna. These students need to hear about your abortion experience. Many could be in the same spot you were back then."

My heart skipped 700 beats with his edict. Dr. Dobson did not realize the concept of addressing those students terrified me. He simply was ensuring my visit included an added spiritual impact of a transparent testimony. Since he was the CEO of the ministry where I worked, I had no other choice but to speak.

Four months later, my heart was racing as we drove onto the campus. My whole body responded negatively. I grew anxious and troubled as deep recollections of events were triggered again.

Many scenes from my past there flashed quickly in front of my eyes. Yet with each "scene" came a deeper understanding of my days on that campus. That helped my ongoing process of forgiving the younger version of myself for making such a choice.

*When the Taylor staff prayed with me before I spoke, God tamed every foreboding.* Peace descended into my heart when I was introduced. You could have heard a pin drop as over 2,000 faces listened in shock as I outlined my abortion experience at that Valentine's Day Chapel in 1997.

It was evident from body language and physical responses that Dr. Dobson was right – *abortion was still possible on that campus.* I was blessed to know those students understood the emotional and spiritual pain of abortion. It was my prayer that hearing my story would prevent them from aborting in any unexpected pregnancy situations.

A decade later I visited the pregnancy center across from the Planned Parenthood where I had discovered my pregnancy, I noticed the gates to this Planned Parenthood clinic were wide open and no protestors were in sight. I asked my husband to drive into the parking lot that bore so many memories years earlier. *I then relived my moments leaving that clinic as a 19-year-old.*

There had been excitement in my heart as I walked out those doors. I felt some joy at the thought of being pregnant. My heart started to dream of motherhood and the fairy tale possibility that my boyfriend might propose now that this truth was verified.

My head then turned to the location where my boyfriend's car had been parked. The distance from the door to the parking lot was exactly as I had remembered. I then recalled his words when he saw my tear-stained face and read my thoughts.

Dashing all my hopes, he had said, "I know what you are thinking, Sydna. You think I might marry you and we can have this baby. Well, you're wrong. I'm not marrying you and you are not having this baby."

I'm grateful that visiting this Planned Parenthood didn't unlock any added stress or anxiety. This boyfriend had long been forgiven for the part he played in my choice. The special gift of this last exposure was viewing the pregnancy center sign from that parking lot, offering women in that community the support to make a better choice than abortion.

### Comforting Scripture

**Philippians 4:6-8** - *Do not be anxious about anything, but in every situation, by prayer and petition, with thanksgiving, present your requests to God. And the peace of God, which transcends all understanding, will guard your hearts and your minds in Christ Jesus. Finally, brothers and sisters, whatever is true, whatever is noble, whatever is right, whatever is pure, whatever is lovely, whatever is admirable—if anything is excellent or praiseworthy—think about such things.*

### Activity

**Discover Your Triggers -** Sit down and review some of the moments in your life that found you anxious/upset and record these in your journal. Write as much of that situation as you can remember. *Be sure to include moments of anxiety where you did not understand why you were upset. Also include situations where you felt like you were certainly crazy.*

After these memories are recorded, add dates to these events. Relate these dates to your abortion timeline that you began in Chapter 1. Then list these dates on your current yearly calendar so that you are aware that that day may be triggering. Make some plans on how to address this day when it arrives. As always, ask for God's help!

## Chapter 4 – Demolishing Shame

When a woman leaves an abortion clinic, one is dead, and one is wounded. The wounded woman typically feels immediate relief. That respite is temporary. The choice has been made and the anxiety, threats and arguments often surrounding such a choice are typically silenced. Most believe they can forget the abortion ever happened.

As the post-abortive journey moves along, trauma often presents itself in ways that seem *unrelated* to abortion grief. It's common for post-abortive women to discount sudden emotional and spiritual pain that appears for no reason. Abortion is rarely discussed as the source for this sudden angst.

When the emotional and spiritual pain arrives, women can also fear they are experiencing God's judgment. They can sadly believe that everything that goes wrong in their life is due to God's wrath over their abortion. Many do not realize that this pain is the *consequence* of abortion – not God's punishment.

One difficult symptom of the Abortion PTSD experience involves **self-destructive behaviors**. Refusing to forgive the younger version of yourself for making such a death choice is where many women find themselves years later. Others simply writhe in pain without their child(ren) to hold and love. Still others will become quite cruel, filled with hate and unable to understand why they cannot be at peace.

Abortion's emotional and spiritual pain is likely one of worst forms of self-torture that exists in our world today. It binds our hearts to the anxiety and shame that someone could discover this awful truth about us and cast us out. Reaching out for help seems impossible as many cannot even speak the word "abortion."

Refusing or rejecting God's healing – *or believing you are unworthy of God's forgiveness* – can certainly enhance abortion's emotional and spiritual damage cycle. The worst aspect of self-destructive behaviors is listening/believing that nasty voice inside your heart that says you deserve to rot in Hell for making this choice.

Self-destructive behaviors can also be encouraged by other abortion antagonists. My own abortion journey involved emotional abuse from my child's birthfather. When he noticed I was sad after our abortion, he threatened to tell everyone about it if I did not "get happy" and stop making him feel bad.

He rebuffed any related guilt, saying, "Abortion is safe and legal. You do not get to mourn a child that you chose to abort. Get happy or I'll make your life even more miserable."

Suffering often becomes a way of life after abortion and that normally includes deep shame. *Women unbelievably remain with abusers because they feel they deserve the punishment for aborting*. Blackmail threats about sharing this secret can be more disabling than strong ropes or walls.

Satan does not have any new tricks. His biggest con job is to remind us of the myth that God will not forgive an abortion decision. God's word, featured below, trashes that lie:

Isaiah 58:9 – *Then you will call, and the Lord will answer; you will cry for help, and he will say: Here am I.*

2 Corinthians 5:17-18 – *Therefore, if anyone is in Christ, the new creation has come: The old has gone, the new is here! All*

*this is from God, who reconciled us to himself through Christ and gave us the ministry of reconciliation....*

Rebuffing tears is another common part of choosing not to heal after abortion. Many women reveal their biggest fear is that if they begin to cry, they will not be able to stop. They stew in anxiety that if they allow themselves to grieve, they may be led to commit suicide.

If the woman did not know God before her abortion, the emotional and spiritual pain may not be as severe. During the salvation experience, however, God often reveals past sins as part of the redemption process. God's spirit is fresh in these hearts and His comfort can be so very tangible.

God can heal abortion's wounded hearts instantly, just as is revealed in Mark 6:56 – *Wherever He (Jesus) entered, into villages, cities, or the country, they laid the sick in the marketplaces, and begged Him that they might just touch the hem of His garment. And as many as touched Him were made well.*

For others, God chooses to walk them through the healing process versus experiencing instant relief. Whatever you may think, God never enjoys watching us suffer. He has a reason for the ache we experience. **God never wastes the pain we endure**. He uses it to heal our hearts.

When God showed me that I had lost a child in my abortion, that revelation was initially overwhelming. I had to cry and could not stop thinking about this child that years earlier I had allowed to die.

Then came the day when I thought I was losing my next child in the womb. Without thinking, I got down on my knees and prayed to God saying, "Please forgive me for my abortion. Do not take this baby to punish me."

That quickly spoken prayer set 1 John 1:9 to work in my heart – *If we* **confess** *our sins, he is faithful and just and will forgive us our sins and purify us from all unrighteousness.*

Within a few minutes of that prayer, I saw my unborn child on an ultrasound screen. God's purification process to remove my unrighteousness began in that moment. My fully human looking child was kicking me and sucking his thumb at sixteen weeks gestation.

I knew then that I had aborted a baby and **not** a blob of tissue as they had described at the abortion clinic. It was an unforgettable moment in my life.

In embracing the pain and agreeing to attend an abortion recovery class, I gave God the keys to my heart. Back then, I really did not have a choice. God was pursuing me by reminding me daily of the unconfessed sin that surrounded my life. In turning back to Him, confessing my sin, and asking Him to help with my current pregnancy, **I had to face the pain of my abortion.**

I then begged God to take away that intense pain. God did not answer that prayer the way I wanted. Because God created me, He knew how to heal my heart. He knew I had to also address the additional sins that had resulted because of my abortion.

When God wants us to come back into His fellowship, *He can use common triggers of abortion pain to wake up the grief in our souls.*

## Removing Abortion Disgrace

If an average of one third of American women have experienced abortion, *why is it that you rarely hear anyone confess to this choice*? Abortion is often cloaked in secrecy. Post-abortive silence speaks volumes about the shame that is often associated with this choice.

In working with tens of thousands of post-abortive individuals, I find it is often most difficult for abortion's wounded hearts to resolve the issue of their post-abortive shame in having participated in abortion. Triggers like the birth of a subsequent child, learning the details of fetal development, losing another child through miscarriage, or a future understanding that they participated in the loss of their own child through abortion can intensify post-abortive shame.

Even if our hearts were coerced or harassed into the abortion decision, many come to the point of recognition that they should have fought harder not to have the abortion. It doesn't matter if these conclusions are accurate or not. Post-abortion emotions can be complicated to understand.

To address this emotional pain, it's important to review the difference between the emotions of guilt and shame:

**Guilt** involves the realization that one has violated the law or the rights of another person and/or God.

**Shame** is remorseful consciousness of guilt that makes one feel disgraced or dishonored.

While guilt tells us we made a mistake, **shame wants to tell us we are a mistake.**

Post-abortive shame often produces thoughts of worthlessness. Many believe they are unworthy of love at any level. This emotion can often lead to suicidal tendencies and deeper depression as we believe we are unworthy of forgiveness.

Unhealthy shame is often called "the sorrow of the world." It can be a major enemy in the effort to healing, especially if it binds us to maintaining secrets. Many can be stunted in their spiritual growth because they expend great energy to ensure, "No one will ever know about my abortion. It will always remain a secret."

Abortion disgrace can initiate great fear of parents, spouses, children, or friends discovering an abortion secret. Even when loved ones show OBVIOUS compassion towards other post-abortive people, it is hard for the post-abortive to believe they even deserve to be accepted and forgiven for this choice.

Women who endure physical, verbal, and emotional abuse at the hands of others often believe they "deserve the abuse" for their abortion action. This form of self-destruction is often the most painful.

Even in professional counseling situations, rarely does an intake form include the questions, "How many abortions have you experienced?" While we may not answer truthfully, simply asking us the question can reveal that our abortion could be the root of our pain.

Pro-choice rhetoric often insists that post-abortive shame is the result of Christian ethics and judgment. Their message outlines that only Christian women feel shame about their past abortions. Even in Japan, with less than 3% of a Christian population, post-abortive women have memorials to their aborted babies in Shinto shrines. While God's hand of conviction may bring the truth of the loss of a child to a clearer level, there is no proof that only Christian women suffer from the emotional, spiritual, psychological, and physical consequences of abortion.

Shame can be deeper for those who chose abortion **multiple** times. These women often believe they are much worse than anyone else. This shame is also complicated when someone remembers one abortion more vividly than another.

Many combat sorrowful emotions by leaning into anger. That fury often results in the hardening of our hearts. Anger rarely resolves the sensation of sadness because we lose the connection to God's grace that helps us heal.

**Why Didn't God Stop Me?**

"I asked God to stop me if aborting wasn't His will for my life. When He didn't, I felt it was okay. Why didn't He stop me, Sydna?" the post-abortive woman asked.

Many faith-based hearts prayed before they aborted, asking for God to intervene if this wasn't His will for them. These ambiguous prayers are often answered, just not in the way we expect.

This woman remembered struggling to find a parking spot near the abortion clinic. She initially thought God was trying to stop her. Then someone pulled out of their spot. "I felt that was God's sign saying abortion was okay," she concluded.

While the actual word "abortion" does not appear in the Bible, Jesus spoke about the beauty of children in Matthew 19:13-14 - *Then people brought little children to Jesus for him to place his hands on them and pray for them. But the disciples rebuked them. Jesus said, "Let the little children come to me, and do not hinder them, for the kingdom of heaven belongs to such as these."*

In discovering my pregnancy in a Planned Parenthood clinic as a teenager, I too prayed for God's direction. I was so steeped in sin and shame by that point, I could not discern any particular response. Opening a Bible was not in my mindset either.

When I entered that abortion clinic, I felt I had an angel on one shoulder speaking into my right ear, and another darker perspective – a devil - addressing my left. The messages were quite different.

Part of me felt the urge to flee. Another part of my heart replayed the typical **abortion logic** – *this was a safe and legal choice for teenagers in my position.* The logical voice won out.

My boyfriend's perspective was replayed upon entering the parking lot. If I came out still pregnant, he stated he would leave me homeless on the streets. Even with his threat, a huge part of my heart knew I was headed for extreme regret if I went through with aborting my child.

In that moment of overwhelming confusion, stress, and uncertainty, it was difficult to discern God's perspective. While I had never heard anyone speak against abortion, my heart belonged to the Creator of the Universe. I knew God loved children.

Had I the courage to flee that scene, I'm confident my Heavenly Father would have had help waiting around the corner. In many cities, that assistance is offered through pregnancy center ministries.

Playing these type of "sign" games with God can be quite confusing in considering abortion. Few understand that God has already outlined His perspective on abortion in Deuteronomy 30:19 – *I call heaven and earth as witnesses today against you, that I have set before you life and death, blessing and cursing; therefore choose life, that both you and your descendants may live.*

Anger towards God for not physically stopping us from aborting is common in the eventual realization of this choice's impact on our lives. *It is a human tendency to hold God accountable for the decisions we make. The Scripture above outlines that God does not support abortion in any situation.*

It very well could be that God **did** send people and circumstances into your life or cause situations to get your attention. Perhaps we simply didn't recognize the help as coming from God?

One woman outlined that she prayed for God's direction. The next day, she drove past numerous billboards that outlined basic pro-life messages like, "Abortion stops a beating heart." These billboards confused her and did not sound like God's answer to her prayer. Her expectations about God giving her a literal "sign" simply wasn't enough to dissuade her.

God gave us the gift of having a free will. By Our Creator's very nature, He does not demand we do things His way, even though it is the best way. God lets us go our own way to make our own choices. Thankfully, He also wants to heal our hearts from all our sins.

Romans 6:23 outlines this truth – *For the wages of sin is death, but the gift of God is eternal life in Christ Jesus our Lord.* God wants every post-abortive person to know that He loves and forgives, no matter what our sin. He speaks to our hearts. The problem is that we often simply don't recognize His voice.

If you are angry at God for not stopping you from aborting, realize that He gave you free choice. Beginning to heal can be as easy as a humble prayer, asking for God's help in understanding your pain.

## Comfort Scripture

**II Corinthians 5:6-10** - *Therefore we are always confident and know that as long as we are at home in the body we are away from the Lord. We live by faith, not by sight. We are confident, I say, and would prefer to be away from the body and at home with the Lord. So we make it our goal to please him, whether we are at home in the body or away from it. For we must all appear before the judgment seat of Christ, that each one may receive what is due him for the things done while in the body, whether good or bad.*

## Activity

**Catalog places, songs and events that were part of your life when you chose abortion**. Listen to some of these songs to see if they do not remind you of additional events during that phase of your life. Visit places that are included on this list – like the school you were attending at the time, an old church, etc. Review the events of those days to gain a physical time frame of when the abortion could have taken place. *Record these memories in your journal for future processing with God.*

## Chapter 5 - Good Grief

Abortion results in death. Since abortion is a choice, society rarely allows post-abortive women the right to grieve their aborted child. Women are expected to get back to living life, like nothing happened. The first step in abortion recovery is simply giving women permission to grieve their aborted child at last and to draw closer to God's comfort.

In the post-abortive journey, expect mourning moments as fresh grief can trigger old grief. As people you love die, grief often returns for your lost child(ren). This is good grief as it allows you to draw closer to God during difficult times of loss when He can comfort your heart at a much deeper level.

With any form of pregnancy loss, the resulting grief can be embraced or denied. In post-abortive hearts, that grief is often *disallowed*. Triggers of abortion pain can ignite sorrow that is difficult to defuse. Once kindled, sorrow can overwhelm and lead the individual to believe they are likely "going crazy."

The first step in addressing the grief is to continue to realize your lost child has always been a real person to God because He is their Creator. While we may have rejected our unborn children as a gift from God, He has always cared for these human beings! There is no sadness in heaven, only peace.

"I was a crying mess all Mother's Day, Sydna," the abortion recovery leader outlined. "This grief crept up on me. I didn't think it would hurt anymore since I have gone through recovery. Will I always cry when I remember this child?"

### Fresh Grief

Encountering fresh grief after an abortion recovery class doesn't mean we are not healed – *just that God isn't finished with us!* God created tears to help us heal. Tears have a biological purpose in helping cleanse our bodies of toxins.

There is also a whole book of the Bible on grief – *Lamentations* – that outlines crying is good for us, whenever it arrives. There are many moments in life when this grief can be ignited as well. These include:

**Holidays** – particularly Mother's Day and Christmas – can summon an emotional impact that often surprises post-abortive people with fresh grief.

**Death of Loved One** – When someone in our life dies – whether due to abortion or after living life on Earth – grief arrives quickly. This "understood grief" then can circle around and remind us of all the people in our lives that have died. These departed loved ones line up in our minds as we go back over the emotions of losing each one all over again.

**Age Comparisons** – Grief returned to my heart, out of the blue, when I asked a new pregnancy center leader her age. Sure enough, she was born within two months of my aborted child's possible due date. I did not comprehend that meeting someone the age of my child would initiate a deeper pain in my heart. By embracing grief and being open to God's help, I was able to ensure the next encounter of someone Jesse's age would be easier on my heart.

**Life Events** – One day I drove by a high school where a graduation ceremony was taking place. I smiled in considering all the families that were present and the celebrations that would ensue afterwards. Out of the blue, I realized that had Jesse been born, he would have been graduating at that time too. Tears overwhelmed me then and I took time to prayerfully consider my grief with that enlightenment.

**Generational Cycles** – Many years after aborting Jesse, I was celebrating the birth of a team member's grandchild. Her son was Jesse's age and beaming in the photo as he held his newborn son. I realized that Jesse could have been providing me with grandchildren. They didn't tell me at the abortion clinic that I'd be grieving lost grandchildren that will never be on Earth because of my abortion!

God keeps track of our tears. David outlines this truth in Psalms 58:7-9 – *Record my misery; list my tears on your scroll — are they not in your record? Then my enemies will turn back when I call for help. By this I will know that God is for me.*

Embracing grief also has a reward, outlined in Psalm 126:4-6 – *Restore our fortunes, Lord, like streams in the Negev. Those who sow with tears will reap with songs of joy. Those who go out weeping, carrying seed to sow, will return with songs of joy, carrying sheaves with them.*

Grief and joy do not seem to go together but they do! I never want to "get over" missing my aborted child or my parents, who are now in heaven. Thinking about them can make me cry or laugh depending on the memory. When expected grief comes, like on their birthdays, anniversary dates or just looking through photos, I can weep again. I miss them. By embracing this grief, I relieve my burden and receive God's warm love.

**Focused grief** means openly embracing any level of potential sorrow in allowing tears to flow freely when they arrive. Whatever triggers abortion grief, realize tears are essential in the ongoing healing process.

Lamentations 2:8-9 shares more on God's purpose in our mourning our aborted children – *The hearts of the people cry out to the Lord. You walls of Daughter Zion, let your tears flow like a river day and night; give yourself no relief, your eyes no rest. Arise, cry out in the night, as the watches of the night begin; pour out your heart like water in the presence of the Lord. Lift up your hands to him for the lives of your children…*

Sometimes we sin and God convicts us. God is very different from the enemy in His messaging system within our hearts. Should the emotions of shame and guilt arrive when tears are shed, recognize those thoughts as toxic. Understand those overwhelming emotions often arrive with spiritual warfare.

Spiritual warfare is an attack that continues through our time on Earth. The enemy loves to upset us. Old shame can then encircle our hearts as the enemy works to lead us back into his prison of pain. God may use conviction to help us understand our sins, but His messages are not designed to remind us of all our past sins.

In battling the enemy, remember the "armor of God" outlined in Ephesians 6:10-17. God wants us to cling to the truth that He is a good God who heals our hearts and doesn't want us suffering. He is righteous as He brings the message of peace and healing from God, along with conviction.

God also develops our faith to help us endure the constant spiritual attack. When we ask Jesus into our hearts (John 3:16), His word is the perfect place to answer all our questions and receive His comfort.

Healing doesn't mean that we will never feel the pain of abortion again. Grief never ends on Earth. Instead, it circles back around, hopefully drawing us closer to God with each wave of emotion.

Tears are not a sign of weakness but a symbol of God's ongoing healing! So go ahead and have a good cry! It will bring you closer to the best Comforter in the world.

## The Benefits of Grief

Before I attended an abortion recovery class, I felt God could just step in miraculously and sweep away all my emotional and psychological pain relating to this choice. When He didn't heal my heart quickly, I felt abandoned again and thought, "Perhaps He has sent the agony as a way to punish me for sacrificing my child on the altar of choice?" I never realized that His plan for my life included facing this deep trauma from my past. The ache wasn't His punishment but simply a consequence of my abortion choice. Addressing the grief would help me heal.

In Psalm 94:12-15 David writes, *Blessed is the man whom You instruct, O Lord, and teach us Your law. That You may give him rest from the days of adversity . . . For the Lord will not cast off His people, nor will He forsake His inheritance. But judgment will return to righteousness, and all the upright in heart will follow it.*

God's instruction helps us walk through the pain of our choices in life. If He simply removes the pain, we may not learn the intimate details of His love, mercy and grace. This pain is something we may need to understand to avoid sinning in the future.

After my abortion I walked away from God's presence. I believed the shameful message in my head that said God would never want me again since I had abandoned one of His incredible gifts of life. Seven long years of running from this pain left me longing to "partake" in His holiness once again.

My abortion had been a step on the road of many dysfunctional activities that needed to be confessed and resolved with God. The "process" of the abortion recovery class ensured that other parts of my heart were open to revelation and healing. These additional issues were a bigger weight than I had ever imagined and important in my ongoing spiritual health.

The only thing to do is to embrace this pain and understand that God is going to use it in our lives. Whatever you may think, God doesn't enjoy watching His children suffer. God will never give us more than we can emotionally handle. I had always been afraid that if I started crying, I would never stop. I thought addressing the pain could lead me to suicide. I was wrong on both points.

Another thing to understand is the pain is *temporary*. While you don't think it will ever go away, there are thousands on the peaceful side of the grief to prove you wrong. We have survived the truth of our choices, grieved our losses, allowed God's love to help us forgive those who harmed us (including ourselves), and come to the point of peace where God can use us to help others.

Have hope that you won't feel this pain forever. Ask God to give you moments of peace to understand His love and discipline. He won't desert you — ever.

### Tears are Valuable to Your Health

Please understand that tears are an important part of healing. Science has proven that emotional tears are the body's way of releasing stress and reducing pain. So there truly is such a thing as good grief!

Biochemist and "tear expert", Dr. William H. Frey II, at the St. Paul-Ramsey Medical Center in Minnesota, discovered that reflex tears are 98 percent water, whereas emotional tears also contain stress hormones which get excreted from the body through crying.

In studying the configuration of tears, Dr. Frey found that emotional tears contained more of the protein-based hormones that act as a natural painkiller. Our body makes these proteins when under stress. Dr. Frey's research confirmed that the body rids itself of these chemicals through tears, explaining why we can just feel "better" after a good cry.

Additional studies also suggest that crying stimulates the production of endorphins, our body's natural pain killer and "feel-good" hormones."

Grief over an aborted child often is triggered by a subsequent death experience. When my friend and neighbor, Dianne, was murdered in 1990, I had to cry. Because she died through murder, I would jump back and forth from deep-seated anger against her killer to massive mourning spells. With each tear, I was reminded of my aborted child.

God triggered my mourning for my aborted child, Jesse, with Dianne's death. When my father and mother passed away, I cried not only them, but for every person or pet missing from my life. Each death experience started renewed mourning for these past losses.

Even at funerals, society is rarely comfortable around hearts that are in deep sorrow. Some mourners can become so overwhelmed with emotion that they cannot speak. Mourning can lead some to make some strange sounds like wailing. While this sound is welcomed in other nations, American society doesn't respond well to these grief noises.

It can also be difficult to weep around others. Deep grieving often is best accomplished in private so that these emotions don't impact the peace of a household.

Adult tears can be difficult for small children to understand. Children *may internalize the adult's grief to the point where they believe they've done something wrong to cause this pain.* Significant others, who cannot fix the pain can add anger to their comments hoping to stop the obvious sorrow from making them uncomfortable.

At some point, grief can overcome an individual like a wave on a beach. It rolls in, knocks you off your feet, and rolls out leaving you breathless. There is rarely a schedule of when the next wave will hit. Many triggers can spawn tears and it is important to express these emotions when they arrive.

Crying reduces our defenses and initiates a deeper emotional strength afterwards. Mourning is an important part of healing. We often just need permission to grieve. Good grief often needs to be encouraged! As Isaiah 61:1-3 outlines, God wants to, *Comfort all who mourn, to console those who mourn in Zion, to give them beauty for ashes, the oil of joy for mourning, the garment of praise for the spirit of heaviness...*

Many combat sorrowful emotions by leaning into anger. That fury often results in the hardening of our hearts. Anger rarely resolves the sensation of sadness because we lose the connection to God's grace that helps us heal.

It does not help that the world puts post-abortive women in one box, stating that our silence about our abortions means we feel "fine" with this choice. Pro-aborts don't understand that post-abortive women typically muzzle their emotions to protect their secret sin from being revealed.

Feelings of sadness can also be interpreted as a sign of weakness. The feminism spirit that helped us walk into an abortion clinic can lead us to recommending abortion to others or protesting to support abortion providers.

Few realize that sorrow is a path to joy. Embracing grief gives value to our lost children and outlines the emotions that need to be processed. Here are four levels of sadness that can hit post-abortive hearts along their journey through life:

# Beyond Regret: Living Victoriously

**Forbidden Sorrow** – Since abortion is a choice, many women perceive they have no right to "grieve" their aborted child. They wrap their tears deep into their souls as they leave abortion clinics and attempt to forge ahead as if nothing happened. When involuntary tears occur, the individual's intellect works to dominate these emotions by linking them to other past traumas.

**Denied Sadness** – With comments like, "My abortion was the best choice I made," women are disregarding any sense of loss that may have arrived in their hearts after abortion. Anger often is used in the denial process which hardens the woman's heart. Many contact our offices stating, "I can't figure out how I became so mean and angry!" Angry hearts are often unable to love, which can lead to an insensitivity, particularly around children.

**Fearful Blues** – During various "life" moments – i.e., births, deaths, moves, transitions, etc. – denial and anger can cease functioning which tosses us into open grief. Even watching a sad movie can initiate extreme crying jags that are misunderstood in our minds, leading us to fear we may be going crazy.

**Repentant Regret** –When post-abortive people finally allow themselves to mourn the child they lost to abortion, God's power returns harmony to our souls. This is outlined in 2 Corinthians 7:10, *Godly sorrow brings repentance that leads to salvation and leaves no regret, but worldly sorrow brings death.*

The benefit of embracing after abortion sadness means that we realize we lost something very special at the abortion clinic. Naming aborted children and having a memorial service for them can release a great deal of shame and guilt from our souls too. The peace that results changes us at a remarkable level, restoring joy and dismantling destructive anger.

## Comfort Scripture

**Psalm 56:8-11** - *Record my misery; list my tears on your scroll - are they not in your record? Then my enemies will turn back when I call for help. By this I will know that God is for me. In God, whose word I praise, in the Lord, whose word I praise – in God I trust and am not afraid. What can man do to me?*

## Activity

**Prayerfully consider talking to those who know about your abortion**. If they are emotionally supportive, ask them about their memories of your abortion event. By asking them questions about this time frame, they can also provide information as well as comfort. Record what they say in some way and add any new information to your Timeline.

## Chapter 6 - Overcoming Abortion Judgment

If you read or hear negative messages that call you a murderer or killer for choosing abortion, remember that you are not alone. To God, your abortion has never been a secret. He loved you then and He still loves you now. His love will never end. He can help you endure. Many "titans" of the Bible (Moses, David, and Paul) were murderers. God can and will still use you.

### The Murderer or Killer Label

The caller shouted in my ear, "How dare she compare her loss to my miscarriage. After all, she MURDERED her child!"

No one had ever attacked me in such a way during a radio interview. The conversation up until that point with the show's host and the director of the local pregnancy center involved a compassionate discussion about PTSD as it relates to abortion.

When we took this call, I had just shared a portion of my own abortion testimony. We compared abortion grief to what many mothers' feel after miscarriage. The hope of God's healing was outlined along with assurances of no judgment and confidentiality if someone wanted to attend the center's abortion recovery program.

With just a few words, *this caller shattered the safety zone we had tried to establish for wounded post-abortive hearts.* In doing so, she highlighted the worst form of judgment that any post-abortive person could expect – she labeled me a "murderer." If I had just received that judgment directly on-air, how could listeners expect to be received if they should make such a confession?

Thankfully, the director responded for me. Calmly and lovingly, she spoke to all listeners about God's grace and mercy. While I can't remember her exact words, I was comforted as was the harsh caller by her words. Clearly, she was in deep pain.

I didn't speak much more, and the interview concluded. Her comment had silenced me quickly. Internally I was fighting the warfare that these comments stirred in my heart. The word "murdered" rang in my head continuously. Guilt was reignited followed by a quick conclusion that I could never be effective for Christ. Shame poured down on my head like a river.

That led to a good cry as I tried to process my emotions. *I was spiritually mature enough to know my negative conclusions were what the enemy wanted me to believe.* I'm sorry to admit I stayed in that zone for a while. This incredibly wounded woman had hurt me deeply. Sometimes it's not that hard to draw blood from my abortion wound, despite the fact it has been healed for many years. I took the rest of the day off.

To compare a young woman heading into an abortion clinic to someone who commits first-degree murder is clearly unsuitable. Neither is the murderer or killer label Christ-like or productive in stopping abortion. Since one third of all American women are post-abortive, those comments have more power to wound on this topic.

In talking to thousands of women over the last 30 years in ministry, *I have never known or heard of a woman who entered an abortion clinic in a truly murderous mindset.* The image of an ISIS terrorist brandishing a knife to a Christian's throat doesn't compare to a young woman who feels she has no other choice but to abort.

# Beyond Regret: Living Victoriously

Abortion rarely brings gleeful thoughts about an unborn child's impending demise. If you have ever waited in the reception area of an abortion clinic as I have, the emotions gravitate towards fear and pain.

I saw a social media post recently that read, *"I was on my way to kill my daughter when some folks pointed me in a better direction..."* While happy with the overall story that the woman did not abort, I was deeply impacted by her use of the word "kill." Like "murder," kill can devastate those hearts that are barely hanging on in this world, believing their own depressed conclusions that they have committed an unforgivable sin and there is no hope for them.

There was a point in my healing where I recognized that I had taken the life of my own child versus a blob of tissue. By that time, God had already prepared the soil around my soul to grasp the truth of my actions. I couldn't blame anyone else. No one dragged me onto that abortion table. I had walked in all on my own, like a lamb to slaughter. I had the ultimate guilt and responsibility. Thankfully, through Christ's ultimate sacrifice along with a local abortion recovery program, I was set free from the bondage of that sin and allowed His peace that passes all understanding into my heart.

I have several people in my life who served prison sentences for first-degree murder. Many were also post-abortive before the time of their crime. While it cannot be blamed entirely, *their abortion trauma was part of the puzzle that led them into other future destructive and dysfunctional behaviors.* Obviously, those behaviors led to criminal activity and then a prison sentence. These individuals helped outline the difference between abortion and planning/murdering a person standing in front of you. Taking the life of a human versus the denial that our child was an actual human are very different things.

The use of these terms in our presence won't stop anytime soon. We need to find a way to cope.

## #ShoutYourAbortion Fallout

*O, The Oprah Magazine* often promotes the hashtag **#ShoutYourAbortion** by featuring the woman's story who started this campaign. This editorial team oddly places this story under the "Inspiration" section of this publication.

This abortion proud hashtag was tweeted over 300,000 times. Whatever the reasons for participating in this promotion, the use of this hashtag can have massive implications for the American family whose members have been lost to abortion.

Let's talk about these women who are proudly proclaiming their abortion truth. First, understand these women did not share this truth publicly to specifically wound you. Many believe that if abortion is safe and legal, why would it upset anyone? Unfortunately, only time can change their perspectives.

Please understand that a typical post-abortion characteristic can be to endorse and even recommend abortion to others in the early days after losing their child. Many encourage abortion as a way of reminding themselves that their choice was a good one. That helps keep pain and grief at bay from impacting their mother's heart – at least for a while.

After my abortion I surrounded myself with pro-choice people whom I felt would not judge me for this choice should they discover my truth. I only supported pro-choice candidates and even encouraged one of my friends to abort. Thankfully, she didn't listen to me, and her daughter is alive and well.

# Beyond Regret: Living Victoriously

The candor of an abortion truth, tweeted quickly and without thought to future consequences, will remain a permanent record of a child's death. It can also be a black mark in some circles for the woman who confessed in such a sensational manner. Once an abortion secret is revealed publicly, it can be used as a reason to discredit the women at many levels for the rest of her life. Sadly, sharing this truth rarely enhances the post-abortive life but often reduces it.

Once you have lost a child to abortion, the experience becomes part of your soul forever. If the abortion remains unconfessed and unhealed, it can fester and grow into either pro- or anti-abortion sentiments.

Few consider the consequences to family and friends who cannot understand a loved one's stance to glorify a choice that cuts off a whole family branch. Anger and outrage typically result towards the post-abortive woman from these family members when they discover an abortion truth.

Participating in the #ShoutYourAbortion campaign has also dredged up many women's vivid experiences in these clinics during their own abortions. These abortion promoting tweets brought back memories many had hoped to forget.

The world is finally learning the dysfunctional impact that can occur in a woman's life due to the "care" of abortion providers who are calloused towards tiny human beings. As major "life issues" like births, deaths, weddings, and funerals occur, these abortion decisions often come back to haunt us.

Two years after my abortion, I was in my last semester of college. Before I met two family members for dinner, I spent twenty minutes talking with fellow students about how abortion empowers women. I was in that "abortion proud" phase when

I sat down to dinner later that evening. Sadly, that meant I wounded two family members.

While it was unplanned, I casually announced to these family members, "I'm so glad that abortion is legal. I would never be to this point in my education without it."

This couple responded in total shock. Anger was the next emotion expressed as one asked fiercely, "You actually had an abortion?"

My response was positive and upbeat because I was in deep denial about the loss of my child's life. I harshly responded, "Yes! It was the best decision of my life."

The emotions these two individuals presented towards me then were unexpected. I had no clue that my abortion truth would be considered a death experience to them.

Heartlessly, I continued to outline why my abortion had been a great choice. As I talked, their anger and opposing sadness increased.

Confused, I grew angry with these people and asked harshly, "Do you think I shouldn't have aborted?"

No answer was given. They simply stood up and left the restaurant abruptly in the middle of dinner. *Never again would these two people sit in my presence without the same emotion of disrespect and hatred being presented towards me.* My casually shared abortion truth shifted their love for me to hatred - permanently.

Seven years later my perspective on abortion changed to the opposite spectrum. It wasn't until I saw my next child fully formed on an ultrasound screen that I "realized" I had lost a person that day in the abortion clinic and not a "blob of tissue." That experience moved me to my knees with great conviction that I had participated in something that took an obvious person's life – my own child.

Once God healed my heart, I became a pioneer in sharing my abortion experience publicly. This testimony outlined how my abortion impacted me negatively at a spiritual, emotional, psychological, and physical level.

Thousands of women who felt the same way about their "choice" responded to this broadcast. My efforts in helping women find healthy ways to grieve this choice and forgive themselves with God's help began with that first public sharing. For the last 30 years, God has used my abortion testimony to help tens of thousands find the same peace after abortion.

Despite the Godly results of healing, there were major costs to my family for this public confession, just like there can be for women who use a #ShoutYourAbortion hashtag.

While my life has drastically changed regarding my support of abortion, it made no difference to these two individuals who understood I had once defended abortion. Even in specifically asking for their forgiveness for both aborting my child and speaking so casually about it to them, *no clemency was given.*

God's grace, mercy and truth applies to every post-abortive person despite the pain they may have caused in other hearts. God can help you to face the anger and outrage that can occur in confessing this sin.

Later God would supernaturally give me an answer as to why one of these family members could not forgive me. After sharing my testimony for a pregnancy center fund-raising banquet, the director asked me an odd question using a name of a woman who had nearly joined our family through marriage. This individual had been in the audience that night and volunteered at the center.

While the director could not share the truth specifically, she stated, "Use your discernment, Sydna. You know that most people join abortion recovery efforts because they have EXPERIENCED abortion. Play that thought out, won't you?"

Suddenly I realized what this director was saying indirectly. The relationship between this woman and my family member had ended due to an abortion. Another family member had been aborted before my Jesse. While that truth was quickly shocking, it also was straight from the hand of God.

I quickly understood this family member's rage against me. A post-abortive person – male or female – who is living in secrecy about this choice typically avoids hearing/seeing or reading anything about abortion. By sharing mine so casually, I had put that individual into a point of resurrecting those emotions quickly. Then when I apologized and outlined my ministry work, I had convicted them even further.

While this discovery helped me forgive this family member by understanding WHY they had rejected me, it also allowed me the time to grieve this other child that was lost in our family. Until God touches this individual's heart, the door between us will remain close.

Whenever someone offers you judgment and rejection due to your abortion truth, take the time to realize they may just have experienced it as well. Use that likelihood to forgive them and pray for them. They certainly need healing too.

## Truth versus Condemnation

"If she isn't comfortable being called murderer, then she's not healed!" the comment outlined on a shared post of my past blog entitled, "I Can Hear You." *You can read my blogs at RamahsVoice.com.*

For many years I've been blogging about elements of the American post-abortive experience, particularly among those who identify as "spiritual." These posts are part of Ramah's mission to offer the hope of God's healing to abortion's wounded through ongoing awareness and outreach.

In this blog, I outlined a time in my early ministry life of sharing my abortion testimony when the woman called that radio show and angrily labeled me a "murderer."

Once the blog posted, the message in several FB comments was clear – *If I could not EMBRACE other people calling me a murderer or killer, then I certainly must not be "healed."*

Since when does being healed involve embracing condemnation from others? We don't call our soldiers "killers" when they return from war. While these veterans may have taken lives in battle, they were under orders to do so and not personally responsible. I have lied in the past, but I would not have found God if I had been called a liar every time someone tried to talk to me.

Let's not confuse speaking the truth with an emphasis on condemnation. Jesus did not brand the woman at the well (John 4) as an adulterer. Instead, He *gently* outlined the truth – *"You have had five husbands and the one you are with is not your husband."* God's love changes hearts, not name calling or making judgmental statements.

Many of us can identify with this Biblical female. She was a Samaritan, a race in those days that Jews utterly despised and believed had no access to their God. She was ostracized and marked as immoral by her community. Jesus unveiled grace to her in a different way from other sinners. He spoke to her as a person of worth and value, despite her moral situation.

Clearly, this woman KNEW she was a sinner. Meeting Jesus when the area was was empty of other people made that obvious. *She waited until the well was empty before coming to draw her water, outlining she obeyed the isolation edict they placed on her as an immoral woman.* God knew she needed to see herself as worthy of His love despite her sins. Only an outcast could understand what a magnificent gift God's love was that day in just a simple conversation with Jesus.

After this encounter, the woman shared the story with her community and many believed in Jesus after she outlined, "He told me everything I ever did." Because of the simple respect and love Jesus offered to a scorned, immoral woman, many lives were touched and enhanced with God's peace.

Personal healing is not up to the scrutiny of others. Only God can judge a person's heart status. By calling my healing into question, these judgmental commenters proved the point I was trying to make in the blog.

As with all toxic comments, they were removed so that the wounded wouldn't take them to heart and remain in their silent prisons of pain! My heart is strong enough to bear these attacks, but readers are at another level entirely.

Post-abortive people, like the woman at the well, don't need condemnation. We are hard enough on ourselves. *Many of us don't believe we DESERVE healing either.* We become spiritually thirsty and yearn for living water that will heal our hearts.

## Steps to Take When You Feel Abortion Judgement

Since abortion is such a VOLATILE topic, it's essential that post-abortive women depersonalize any negative comments they hear related to this issue. In this section we will outline how to reject condemnatory speech relating to abortion.

**Depersonalize the Attack** – When a stranger yells at me after I've shared my abortion testimony, I always realize that they don't know me well enough to hate me personally. They hate abortion and I've likely triggered them in some way.

There will always be people that are harsh towards women who abort. Realize that they likely are grieving a child that someone else aborted. Their emotions are unchecked and misunderstood in their hearts which often leads to angry responses upon hearing the term "abortion." While it may seem like they hate you personally, they simply cannot because they don't know you at all. Take that truth into your heart when feeling demoralized.

People often believe every single one of us aborted in a *murderous mindset*. They perceive we were like serial killers, enjoying the destruction that abortion brings. These hearts then conclude we are *unredeemable*.

These unknowing people will always be with us. Lean into God's grace and mercy when these opinions hit your world. He doesn't agree with those conclusions!

**Understand Accusers Can Be Post-Abortive** - Abortion judgment often comes from closeted post-abortive individuals. The last thing most listeners consider is that the individual shouting the hardest against abortion is normally one that has experienced it! If they do not confess to their own abortion, they can certainly rattle an audience to hate our kind!

Before my abortion healing, I was terrified that someone may just KNOW that I had done this to my unborn child. Simply hearing the "a" word threw me into guilt and shame. The anger would then arrive to help me offset the unexpressed grief in my heart for my lost child. I became extremely self-righteous in that anger and condemned others for their pro-life stance while never sharing my own abortion secret. *I believed that when someone was against abortion, they were against me as well!*

God verified this truth MANY times but particularly when I discovered my disparaging family member was also post-abortive. *Those outside of God's healing can be our own worst enemies.* While the pro-life movement can certainly be judgmental, they are not usually as vehement in their comments toward us unless they have an unhealed abortion wound.

Keep this in mind when your anger and guilt is triggered by negative comments relating to abortion. The following passage, found in I Timothy 1:12-17, can help your heart. God had a plan in healing your abortion pain just like He did with Paul, a former mass murderer of Christians. This passage is entitled, ***The Lord's Grace to Paul:***

*I thank Christ Jesus our Lord, who has given me strength, that he considered me trustworthy, appointing me to his service. Even though I was once a blasphemer and a persecutor and a violent man, I was shown mercy because I acted in ignorance and unbelief. The grace of our Lord was poured out on me abundantly, along with the faith and love that are in Christ Jesus.*

*Here is a trustworthy saying that deserves full acceptance: Christ Jesus came into the world to save sinners—of whom I am the worst. But for that very reason I was shown mercy so that in me, the worst of sinners, Christ Jesus might display his immense patience as an example for those who would believe in him and receive eternal life. Now to the King eternal, immortal, invisible, the only God, be honor and glory for ever and ever. Amen.*

Those in political leadership that advocate for abortion rights are typically post-abortive. Before my healing, I worked to advance abortion rights. It seemed that I needed to do this to prove to myself that my abortion had been a GOOD decision. Whenever I stood up for abortion, God would convict my heart and unleash pain to the point where I would become silenced. If I couldn't stop myself, He would do so for me.

I volunteered for a certain political campaign in college. They gave me a script to read when making phone calls that included demonizing those that stood for life. The first call I made found me completely mute when I hit that line in the script on abortion. I could not speak at all and hung up. Feeling foolish, I dropped out of that campaign. That was a good thing!

Many post-abortive women in political leadership don't have God's voice in their hearts to convict them. They simply rattle off horrible things about their abortion that enable society to hate us all to a larger extent! Focus on the fact that God knows the truth and is the only real judge in the end.

**Society Puts Weights on Certain Sins but God Does Not -**
While abortion may feel like the absolute worst sin we could have chosen, God doesn't see it that way. He views ALL sin the same. A white lie will receive the same judgment in heaven as an abortion as revealed in I John 5:17-18:

*All wrongdoing is sin… We know that anyone born of God does not continue to sin; the One who was born of God keeps them safe, and the evil one cannot harm them.*

Tiny sins are the same as great sins in God's eyes. Thankfully, God sees our hearts and our motivations with this sin in repenting of it. He saw your heart during your days of choosing abortion. He sees your heart as it is today.

Each morning I wake up I ask God to help me not to sin that day. While I still can sin, God's conviction arrives rapidly. In confessing when I feel convicted, God's peace returns to my heart.

If you are participating in any overt sin, please stop. Realize that God wants you to enjoy His presence which is often curtailed when we chose to sin, sending us down the wrong road. It's just not worth it, no matter how small that sin seems to your heart.

## Comforting Scripture

**Psalm 130:6-8** – *My soul waits for the Lord, more than those who watch for the morning—yes, more than those who watch for the morning. O Israel, hope in the LORD; for with the LORD there is mercy, and with Him is abundant redemption.*

## Activity

Sit down with a piece of paper that starts **Dear (your name)** and ends with **Love, God**. Ask God to help you through this letter writing. Then pick up a Bible and randomly open it and read the first verse that you see! Be sure to record how it impacted your heart!

## Chapter 7 – Dynamics of Sharing the Secret

Being bound to secrets is a troubling thing, especially when our children could repeat our same mistakes. God must lead you in the details of sharing this secret. If there is someone in your life whom you are afraid to talk about your abortion, start in prayer.

Sharing this truth can open a lot of doors to healing a relationship and preventing abortion from being chosen in future generations. Transparency and genuineness are powerful and will be a part of the freedom from the past you desire.

One thing I ask women who are apprehensive about sharing their abortion story is this – *"If a woman walked up to you and said she was going to abort and asked for your opinion, would you share your abortion story with her?"*

Nine times out of ten, these hearts will instantly provide positive responses. Of course they would share their secret privately to spare this woman and her child the horrors of abortion.

Sharing your secret privately in a pregnancy center ministry with someone who is considering abortion can truly be an incredibly effective way to stop abortion. However, most are quite scared to share this secret with the world at large. In this chapter, we will outline many aspects of sharing this secret to help you determine how God is leading you on this topic.

### Four Costs of Sharing an Abortion Secret

As one of the first women to publicly confess my abortion secret in 1992 on a radio broadcast that reached millions, I did not count the costs of sharing this secret. God had placed me at the top of the food chain for pro-life efforts at Focus on the Family in 1991. That was no coincidence. He obviously had a plan to use my sin to help others not only make a better choice than abortion but find His healing afterwards.

To whom God calls, He also empowers. Just understand that He may NOT be calling you to speak publicly about this loss. God's leading in those early days was obvious and my organization encircled me with support at an emotional, spiritual, and physical level. Yet even today, my level of sharing this secret is a RARE calling.

I've shared my story in front of 750,000 people and audiences of one. Each time I re-experience the horror of my abortion, relive my child's violent death and outline God's healing touch. Emotions often fill my heart, but they rarely overwhelm me after all these years. Afterwards, meeting people who have a new understanding of how abortion devastates women is a blessing.

Today there are active efforts by pro-choice and pro-life groups to encourage women to share their abortion stories. These campaigns are designed to get women sharing to NORMALIZE an abortion experience and reduce any related stigma.

Sadly, in sharing this tale *prior to God's healing*, more traumas can result for everyone involved. There are several costs to count before sharing this secret in public. These include:

**The Impact on Implicated Parties** – An abortion decision rarely involves just one person. It is often a "shared" sin that involves other influencers with varying degrees of guilt. The potential father(s) of the child(ren) along with friends and family are often deeply engaged in the decision, perhaps working both for and against this choice. "Outing" these individuals in public can wound these players.

If God is calling you to share, it's best to have conversations with these individuals first. After I recorded that first broadcast, I sent out 25 recordings to impacted people. I found Alan's parents address and sent it to them as well. Out of the 25 sent, only two responded. These two women were mighty prayer warriors who encouraged me. The others didn't really matter as I had simply covered the base and gave them warning. Their response was not required for the show to go on the air.

**The Potential for Genuine Rejection** – The consequences of obedience for the confessor can be difficult for the non-post-abortive to imagine. This level of rejection is not for the faint of heart or spiritually weak.

Luke 7:36-39 outlines the way many dismiss those that are obviously sinful: *When one of the Pharisees invited Jesus to have dinner with him, he went to the Pharisee's house and reclined at the table. A woman in that town who lived a sinful life learned that Jesus was eating at the Pharisee's house, so she came there with an alabaster jar of perfume. As she stood behind him at his feet weeping, she began to wet his feet with her tears. Then she wiped them with her hair, kissed them and poured perfume on them. When the Pharisee who had invited him saw this, he said to himself, "If this man were a prophet, he would know who is touching him and what kind of woman she is—that she is a sinner."*

People have walked out in the middle of my profession of aborting my child with looks of great disdain upon their faces. One person's vocal proclamation over me was horrifying – "Your abortion RUINED you! I will not sit here and listen to you justify the death of your child." Likely, as we have discussed, she is also post-abortive. She missed the entire point as I clearly took on the full weight of that sin in outlining how wrong I had been.

Her reaction has been mirrored by many others over the years. Even at the large ministry where God was moving and shaking, many would see me in their path and turn and walk in a different direction. Their disdain of me was obvious and there was nothing I could do or say to change their minds. I believe my presence simply convicted many of their own unconfessed sins.

Thankfully, Jesus addressed the judgmental Pharisee in Luke 7:44-47 – *Then he turned toward the woman and said to Simon, "Do you see this woman? I came into your house. You did not give me any water for my feet, but she wet my feet with her tears and wiped them with her hair. You did not give me a kiss, but this woman, from the time I entered, has not stopped kissing my feet. You did not put oil on my head, but she has poured perfume on my feet. Therefore, I tell you, her many sins have been forgiven—as her great love has shown. But whoever has been forgiven little loves little."*

**The Consequence to Our Families** – While my mother never knew I was pregnant – or had any involvement in my abortion decision – she felt my public confession was telling the world that she was a bad mother. She never embraced God's calling on my life or my ministry efforts during her time on Earth. Thankfully, the fruit of God's efforts through me is obvious to her now in Heaven. I never realized that my sharing this sin would cause her such deep pain.

My husband and children have been directly impacted. This calling has set them apart in many circles. My son's basketball dreams were squelched by a high school coach whose wife was on the board of the local Planned Parenthood. Despite being an excellent player, this Coach simply benched my son for the call God put on my life. Thankfully, God had other blessings in store for the impact on my children's lives and they have been always proud of my efforts to end abortion one life at a time and help women find God's healing afterwards.

**Deeper Pain** – God used Revelations 12:10-11 to confirm His leading to share this secret in the public arena – *Then I heard a loud voice in heaven say: Now have come the salvation and the power and the kingdom of our God, and the authority of his Messiah. For the accuser of our brothers and sisters, who accuses them before our God day and night, has been hurled down. They triumphed over him by the blood of the Lamb and by the word of their testimony; they did not love their lives so much as to shrink from death.*

Standing in a public spotlight, confessing to taking the life of their child, is not a call that many can embrace. It requires extensive depth, strength, and maturity in God. *Publicly sharing a past abortion must be a clear call from God that can only come after His healing process is complete.*

Some pro-life groups have "used" the testimony of unprepared and unhealed post-abortive individuals to further their own political gain or to raise funds for their pro-life efforts. Without directing them to a healing program, or verifying their attendance, these pro-life efforts can intensify the pain and solitude before discovering God's healing.

There are many women today who are fully equipped by God to share this secret sin. If you are post-abortive, please don't feel pressured to share before God has called and enabled you with His deep healing.

## What's Abortion, Mom?

Abortion is a word that is spoken often today. It is difficult to watch the news or view a movie without abortion being included. For many post-abortive people, just hearing this term can produce anxiety.

Observant children often feel their parent's unease and work to discover what could have set them off. It doesn't take long to realize the root of this apprehension relates to the unknown term of abortion.

Poignant questions from children about deep issues often come out of the blue. When an innocent child asks about abortion, most adults struggle to share this difficult truth. Childlike innocence is shattered quickly when they discover adult truths.

*"Abortion is when they take the baby out of their Mommy's tummy before it is big enough to live. The baby goes back to heaven with Jesus and the mother is often very sad,"* I shared with my middle son when he asked about abortion at the tender age was of seven.

His expression changed in an instant. He responded to this horrifying truth by saying, "Oh, Mom! I'm so glad you didn't abort me!"

My abortion nine years earlier smacked me in the face with his response. I knew that my son needed time to fathom that abortion was legal in his world before going deeper and discovering his mother had chosen abortion for his big brother. I let God lead and did not reveal my own abortion to him then.

Sharing the truth about abortion can bring children to ask more probing questions. This is often where deeper truths about their parents past choices can be discerned, even if the child is young.

When children's questions about abortion come out of the blue, guilt often flashes on their parent's face, further confusing the young interrogator. If the parent shuts down or turns away from the conversation, the child is left confused.

In those moments, children can suspect the worse. After I told my oldest son about my abortion, he would ask me many questions in the following days. For example, he wanted to know if I could have AIDS or if his father was REALLY his dad.

I took the time to give my son direct attention when I heard the word AIDS, outlining my sexual past in the gentlest way possible. God had told me to be prepared so I thought through his potential questions and had responses. Those future conversations were precious and the maternal bonding with each of my children was advanced.

When questions go unanswered, children often jump to conclusions. Kids can easily consider that their parent may have considered aborting them too. Others will develop imaginary friends that could be considered lost siblings from heaven.

After my middle son had time to process this word, and ask many follow-up questions, I didn't want him to wonder about my past.

Six months after his first question, I told this son about my abortion. I shared that I had been a teenager, unaware that abortion was bad. I gently asked for his forgiveness in sending his big brother back to Jesus before he had a chance to live on this earth.

My seven-year-old's response was precious – "Of course I forgive you, Mommy. Wow, I have a big brother in heaven! How cool! What's his name?"

"His name is Jesse," I answered. "Jesus is the greatest parent a child could ever have. I know you and I will meet him someday."

The word "abortion" became a presence in our home life because of my work. It was essential for each of my children to hear my abortion truth from my soul. Thankfully, God went before me and prepared each of their hearts.

When my three sons knew about Jesse, he became part of our family just like any other deceased member. Jesse was not forgotten but grieved and missed by everyone related to him. That was the healthiest part of our family's healing of this difficult pregnancy loss. Abortion became a personal issue to each of my children. God has used them to comfort many hearts after abortion.

Many parents could have briefly considered aborting a child that is now alive and well. When that child begins to ask probing questions after learning about abortion, it is important that the parents heal from those moments of deliberation where death was considered. They can be prepared with a healthy response like the following:

*"There was a time when I found out I was pregnant with you that I was afraid. I considered an abortion but thankfully made a better decision. I cannot imagine what my life would be like without you. God knew all your days and I'm so happy He gave you to me!"*

## The Generational Cycle of Abortion

God's word is clear about confessing secret and shameful choices as again revealed in II Corinthians 4:2 – *Rather, we have renounced secret and shameful ways; we do not use deception, nor do we distort the word of God. On the contrary, by setting forth the truth plainly we commend ourselves to everyone's conscience in the sight of God.*

In assisting both abortion-vulnerable and post-abortive individuals for the last 30 years, I've noticed clear trends in post-abortion behavior across generations. *Post-abortive people often become post-abortive grandparents and great-grandparents when the younger generation follows their same path in life.*

Psalm 78:5-6 outlines God's mindset in educating future family generations about generational sin – *He (God) decreed statutes for Jacob and established the law in Israel, which he commanded our ancestors to teach their children, so the next generation would know them, even the children yet to be born, and they in turn would tell their children. Then they would put their trust in God and would not forget his deeds but would keep his commands.*

The benefit of sharing an abortion truth personally is revealed in Proverbs 14:25 – *A truthful witness saves lives, but a false witness is deceitful.*

The best part of sharing my abortion story with my children was describing how God restored my heart and life. As a family, we experienced Isaiah 38:19 – *The living, the living— they praise you, as I am doing today; parents tell their children about your faithfulness.*

## Silent No More

It was a lonely spot being the first women to pioneer sharing an abortion testimony on a public platform. When I taped my first broadcast for a major Christian ministry in 1992, I had just opened my heart to look at my past abortion pain.

God made it obvious to my heart soon after beginning my job at Focus on the Family that He wanted me to share my personal struggle with abortion to offer the same hope of God's healing to other wounded hearts. I must confess that sharing publicly wasn't a calling I initially embraced. I fought this calling, but God's hand was heavy upon my heart.

While I feared rejection and judgment, the first audience to hear my story responded with love and compassion. Their love gave me the confidence to keep speaking.

Another source of joy was discovering the work of pregnancy centers. Had I walked into a life-affirming pregnancy center for a free pregnancy test, I might not have made my abortion decision. Over 2,400 centers around the U.S. offer tangible services so that women could have more choices than just abortion!

When I first started sharing about my abortion, nothing magical happened. By that time, I was nearly 30 years old with a loving husband who encouraged my public sharing. My parents were mortified, however. The intense pressure of their embarrassment only drew me closer to God to determine if sharing this testimony was His real will for my life.

With a series of confirmations, I continued to share in hopes of reaching other post-abortive women in similar pain. Thankfully, God took care of my parents during that difficult period, providing comfort and support and eventually brought healing to our family.

Many post-abortive people express this calling to share their abortion stories as a desire to break free from their self-imposed prison of secrecy and become "silent no more." This phrase originated with a book by that title. This publication outlined post-abortion pain by sharing anonymous testimonies of those who had chosen abortion.

The stories in that book allowed me to understand that my pain was typical. Many of my apprehensions in life could be related to my abortion choice. I then warily enrolled in an abortion recovery program offered through my local pregnancy center.

Through the love of that pregnancy center, I experienced God's miraculous healing, releasing me from the emotional pain that had haunted my life since my abortion decision. Spiritual maturity is essential as each time I share, I relive my abortion experience.

Ramah International currently does not recommend post-abortive women join **any** post-abortion awareness groups that have any political agenda. However, we lovingly support the work of pregnancy centers, and a few select organizations that labor diligently to empower individuals who have received God's calling to responsibly share their abortion testimony.

Through Christ-centered abortion recovery outreach programs, many individuals are embracing this healing and being mentored to make a difference in the lives of others considering this choice or who are struggling with their own abortion experience.

## Respecting an Abortion Secret

"I was wondering if you would help connect me with anyone that would be willing to share their abortion story and speak into the darkness about our hope in Jesus?" the writer asked.

I quickly determined not to help this individual. Her reasons for a project that encourages women to share the hope of God's healing after abortion were good. *She just needed more help than I could provide which was a distraction to our own busy ministry efforts.*

Another reason for not helping her is that I do not know this individual. *She could easily be pro-abortion, despite using the name Jesus in the message.* Does she have any healing credential to know when women should and should not share their secret? Why doesn't she plow her own ground by helping women around her heal and then using that fruit to find a story or two?

Wanting to help others share their abortion stories doesn't mean individuals have unhealthy motives. To ask another leader to introduce them to women whom they have painstakingly assisted from the depths of abortion's horrifying impact indicates a lack of spiritual warfare understanding.

## Don't Share Your Abortion Story with the Liberal Media

Every so often, the liberal New York Times and other media outlets will ask women to write about their abortions and submit them for potential publication. Here is a common lure they use:

*"We want to hear from women around the World about abortion. We know abortion can be hard to talk about, even with loved ones. But sharing your experience can help others*

*think through the complexities. If you have ever considered an abortion, please tell us about it. We may publish a selection of the responses. We will reach out to you before using your comment or name."*

Think through the complexities of abortion? What does that even mean? Matthew 7:6 reveals God's perspective on this idea – *Do not give dogs what is sacred; do not throw your pearls to pigs. If you do, they may trample them under their feet, and turn and tear you to pieces.*

The abortion industry features abortion as a private choice. Then they work to exploit post-abortive women into submitting their abortion stories for the sole purpose of advancing abortion rights. These pro-abortion groups want to normalize the abortion experience so that it will never become illegal.

It's not rocket science to know that when a fox is watching the hen house, chickens get eaten. *Women who contribute truthful and heartfelt tales of their abortion pain will likely never be published due to this publication's hard stand on abortion rights.* Instead, writers may even be personally cataloged into a liberal database as "anti-abortion."

Being included in such a directory could result in all sorts of liberal outrage against the wounded individual. With ongoing "fake" news and witch hunts, most media outlets have been identified with a liberal bias. They simply cannot be trusted with matters of the heart.

If post-abortive people are singled out among liberals, they typically are attacked or simply discredited by other voices. At the very least, these heartfelt submissions will be rendered worthless as truth rarely is published in liberal media outlets.

To make matters worse, prolife groups often encourage women to submit their stories with liberal fake news outlet. Their "vision" for this task typically is their hope that if enough women respond negatively about the impact of abortion on their lives, they might change people's opinion on abortion.

This mindset is naïve. A compilation of "abortion stories" in 2013 showed the New York Times published 89% of stories from women *who were happy* with their abortion experience. The other 11% of the stories were from women who were working to say this choice was a good experience. *None of the stories outlined the deep regret that often follows this choice.*

Post-abortive women in penance mode often believe they might feel better if they submit their stories. Rarely do these declarations or stories provide relief – only God can do that!

If healing has yet to be established, the emotional impact of compiling 250-500 words about one of the worst days of their lives can be staggering. Afterwards, many hearts simply have no one to help them with the pain this writing can resurrect.

Here are several additional reasons not to submit an abortion story to any public media outlet:

**The written word can endure for generations**. Published words have a very different power over a spoken declaration. I never write something that I am not comfortable with being featured in a Google search. Nor do I allow others to control the words I have written because their edits may change my entire meaning.

**The written word, *even when outlined with great care*, can be easily misunderstood and misused**. Because my childhood experience was devastating, I am careful not to sin further by outlining anything that could wound my family further.

**These assignments can spark new hidden areas of pain**. I have comforted many hysterical post-abortive women whose pain has exploded after completing these written tasks. They may have completed an abortion recovery program but there are other areas of their heart that need deeper healing before they ever go public.

**We cannot trust any organization that currently collects these stories** – even if they are against abortion. With each shift in leadership, organizations change – for the better or for the worse. Promises made by previous leaders may not carry forward to new leaders.

**Published submissions result in the individual's name and abortion story appearing whenever the individual's name is "googled."** Consider the pain that could occur if a family member, who was unaware of this person's abortion, discovered such a "confession" in a public format?

It is too risky to trust the written words of tender post-abortive hearts to anyone who may not have their best interests at heart. Placing the unprepared and/or unhealed post-abortive individual on abortion's battle line by pushing them to submit their abortion story to a liberal outlet is like sending a toddler to war armed with a machine gun! *The potential for self-inflicted wounds and/or injuring allies through "friendly fire" is monumental!*

It is essential that women receive good training and healing before stepping on the public stage with an abortion secret. If you feel God is calling you to speak about your abortion or help others, review Sharing Your Secret – Module 9 on HerChoicetoHeal.com. These nine lessons outline steps to take before sharing and much more. This module can help confirm God's leading on your life or release you from the public speaking task.

The most effective sharing is with those who are considering abortion. Seek out fellowship at your local pregnancy center to see how they can use your story at a one-on-one level with their clients. Their training and spiritual covering will help grow your understanding of how abortion impacts women.

Abortion is simply too volatile of a subject for anyone to address lightly. The point you must keep in mind is Paul's exhortation to Timothy in I Timothy 6:20-21: *Timothy, guard what has been entrusted to your care. Turn away from godless chatter and the opposing ideas of what is falsely called knowledge which some have professed and in so doing have wandered from the faith.*

It is amazing to hold a child that was saved from abortion because God used you to share your abortion truth with their parent(s). That is the best use of an abortion testimony!

**When You Shouldn't Share This Secret**

In first realizing your abortion wound, it's best to take time in prayer asking God who to turn to for help. Those who assisted with your abortion decision are not the best to help you because you could trigger their guilt/shame/grief. They may respond poorly as a result.

One woman shared she had read my book while caring for her dying mother. Her mother could no longer communicate. This dear woman wanted to share about her child in heaven, whom her mother would meet shortly. Since that was impossible, she simply prayed for God's help.

A strange thing then happened. Her mother kept repeating a number. There was no other communication but her continuously repeating this number.

After about ten minutes, the woman felt led to open my book, *Her Choice to Heal: Finding Spiritual and Emotional Peace After Abortion.* She went directly to the page that was the number her mother had been repeating.

On that page, she found several comforting points and a Scripture that provided deeper comfort. Feeling this was no coincidence, she thanked her mother. Her mother then stopped repeating the number. She passed on into heaven a day later.

This dear woman was blessed that God had helped her mother communicate in a way that led her to deeper peace. The experience was a blessing.

Elderly folks that are near death may be unable to emotionally endure the shock of discovering a past abortion. Young children may be too immature to understand this truth as well. God will always lead you so remember to wait upon His direction and ask for His confirmation. He knows the road ahead and will lead you according to His will!

### Comfort Scripture

**Philippians 2:1-3 -** *Therefore if you have any encouragement from being united with Christ, if any comfort from his love, if any common sharing in the Spirit, if any tenderness and compassion, then make my joy complete by being like-minded, having the same love, being one in spirit and of one mind. Do nothing out of selfish ambition or vain conceit. Rather, in humility value others above yourselves,*

## Activity

**Ask God to reveal more memories in His perfect time**. As our Creator, God knows all the details. Through the comfort of His Holy Spirit, memories can spring forth gently. Cocooned memories can be released slowly, like layers of an onion, so they do not overwhelm us because God is in control.

Start in prayer and ask God for His help in remembering the moments of your life that occurred around the abortion. Writing these memories down can unleash more understanding in your heart and lead to a deeper recall of those moments in your life for better understanding.

## Chapter 8 - Deeper Forgiveness

Deeper forgiveness from God, toward yourself, and towards others is essential to the healing process. It is part of the great gift God longs to give you. It is the key to spiritual and emotional freedom that is available from Him. Pray and ask God to reveal to your heart whom you need to forgive. Obedient unconditional forgiveness allows the giving and receiving of God's healing for you.

**God's Forgiveness After Abortion**

"The pastor said my abortion is an unforgivable sin because I blasphemed the Holy Spirit in rejecting His gift of life," a post-abortive woman outlined in an e-mail message. "There is no hope for me to ever enter Heaven, Sydna, right?"

The wounded woman's pastor used Mark 3:28-30 to make his point – *Assuredly, I say to you, all sins will be forgiven the sons of men, and whatever blasphemies they may utter; but he who blaspheme against the Holy Spirit never has forgiveness, but is subject to eternal condemnation…*

In the depths of self-loathing that often results after abortion, many believe ungodly messages that twist this sin into the unforgivable category. Sadly, nothing could be further from the truth.

If you have experienced abortion, God already knows about your choice. You can't surprise Him with that truth. He not only knows what you did, He was there by your side when it happened.

When your child was conceived, God was there.

When you took that positive pregnancy test, God was there.

When you couldn't sleep, or maybe panicked and planned, He was there.

Maybe you didn't hear His voice then? Maybe your fears drowned it out? Or perhaps you closed your ears and didn't listen as He put events, people, or signs in your way to discourage this choice. God knew you'd choose abortion and He stayed with you. His love continued.

God wants to forgive us. He sent His own Son, Jesus Christ, to earth to take on our sin burden so that we could receive His full forgiveness (John 3:16). God hears our intimate thoughts and knows everything we are thinking and feeling. He sees our struggling, tender side reaching out to Him for mercy. He also knows the brutal hearts that persecute others with false messages about His nature.

Eternal condemnation doesn't occur in hearts who turn to God in repentance. What cannot be forgiven is the personal sin (and its effects) on the person who dies *without repenting.*

A sinner who is a subject of eternal condemnation is an enemy of God. They actively work to destroy the good in favor of the evil. *To repent and turn to God after any sin means you are not that level of sinner.* The remorseful are seeking God and actively working to sin no more. *Therein lies the difference.*

The Apostle Paul's life is a perfect example of God's ability to forgive any sin. Prior to finding Christ, Paul killed Christians with incredible brutality. On the Damascus Road (Acts 9), Paul meets God who changes his heart forevermore.

Paul's words from I Timothy 1:16 outline God's reasoning in forgiving him. He was forgiven so that Christ Jesus might, *"display his unlimited patience as an EXAMPLE for those who would believe on Him and receive eternal life.*

In Luke 7:47, Jesus made an obvious point. The judgmental Pharisee was looking upon the "sinful woman" with disdain. He said, *"…her many sins have been forgiven – for she loved much. But he who has been forgiven little loves little."*

Because post-abortive people have been forgiven a great debt of sin, they can love others at a deeper level. Even if God never calls them to share this secret, His mercy changes each person so His loving light of hope can shine through their heart. He can then use us to inspire others to accept His love and live a greater life.

There is NO sin that God cannot forgive. Ask Him, with a humble heart, for His help. God can redeem this sin and change your life – just like He did in my life.

Perhaps you are holding judgment against another, believing them to be "unforgivable," particularly since they chose abortion? Do you understand this is sin? Matthew 5:21b-22 outlines *… anyone who murders will be subject to judgment.'* *But I tell you that anyone who is angry with a brother or sister will be subject to judgment.*

## Forgiving Jane Roe: Abortion's Secondary Impact

"Can I have a cigarette first?"

Norma McCorvey, the infamous "Jane Roe" in the Roe v. Wade case that legalized abortion in America on January 22, 1973, stood next to me behind the stage at Focus on the Family.

This was one of Miss McCorvey's first speaking excursions in the pro-life realm since accepting Christ – a 700-person conference for pregnancy center workers at Focus on the Family in February of 1998. Her request for a cigarette outlined her apprehension of what would happen over the next few minutes.

"There is no time, Miss Norma," I answered. "It will be okay. I'll be standing next to you the whole time."

She gave me a hug of appreciation and outlined, "These people from pregnancy centers are my heroes, Sydna. I hope they don't hate me for making abortion legal. Is it okay for me to just talk to God when I pray?"

"Whatever way God leads you, Miss Norma, is fine," I responded quietly. "Our audience will embrace you deeply. They are excited to hear from you. You'll find love and acceptance here, just as I have as a post-abortive woman."

Miss Norma's book, *Won By Love*, had been published just six weeks earlier. This publication outlined her recent salvation experience which transformed her from abortion clinic worker to pro-life speaker. Miss Norma would later start a non-profit ministry called "Roe No More."

A few minutes later, Miss Norma's message through her prayer was gentle and simple – *Help us, God, save these children from abortion. Forgive me for not doing more sooner.*

Later she would confide to me, "I feel so responsible. Being part of the Roe v. Wade decision made me the face of abortion. It's been an incredible weight for my soul, but God carries my burdens now!"

While Miss Norma never had an abortion – and placed her baby for adoption – she had a good idea about my personal abortion pain. She offered me a rare comfort in saying, "I'm so sorry, Sydna."

# Beyond Regret: Living Victoriously

Accepting Miss Norma's apology for her role in legalizing abortion was an easy way for her to pass this apology onto other post-abortive people. I comfort every reader today that this notorious "Jane Roe" cared deeply for women enduring post-abortion pain and was sincerely sorry that she ever took part in the Supreme Court decision that legalized abortion on demand at all stages of pregnancy.

Secondary abortion pain can result when someone is impacted by another's abortion decision. Whether the person encouraged or fought against this choice makes a difference in how this pain will be processed in years to come.

Those who urge a woman to abort are typically the ones that receive the most hatred, responsibility and blame afterwards from the newly post-abortive person. Anger and hatred are often the first defense against post-abortion tears of grief. Conversely, those who told us not to abort are often the ones that we reach out to when the grief can no longer be denied.

In leaving the abortion clinic where my child died, my personality changed abruptly. The boyfriend who had coerced my child's death met me at the door, picked me up and twirled me around saying, "Oh, Sydna! I thought they had killed you up there."

His relief that I was still alive blew me away. I screamed as his embrace hurt me physically. In processing his comment, I realized suddenly that I could have died during that procedure. I then thought, "What other consequences could there be?"

Then I encountered full blown outrage against this 21-year-old man who had been my child's father. He thought they were killing me but had waited in the car. Dark anger inside of me turned against him then.

It was essential in my abortion recovery healing eleven years later to forgive my child's father. That was just as important as being able to receive Miss Norma's heartfelt apology. God was processing my healing through forgiveness, which ended the rage and pain that surrounded me.

Again, there is no sin that God cannot forgive. After abortion, we are often unable to forgive ourselves for allowing our child(ren) to die. We need God's help to pardon the *younger versions of ourselves* for making such a horrible choice. Those who experience regret for being part of another person's abortion decision often need to follow that same process for peace.

Miss Norma entered heaven in February of 2017. Her burden in connection with the legalization of abortion is gone. Her words of comfort will always be remembered.

**Stranger at the Abortion Clinic**

"This is an abortion clinic! What is she doing here?" I thought as a stranger entered the room. "She does not look like a person who should be having an abortion."

The girl resembled a preppy teenager with short red hair and clear pale skin. "Likely a college student who didn't use contraception," I assumed, judging her.

Bright red splotches appeared over her neck revealing her obvious stress and discomfort in this dark environment. She walked like a terrified lamb, obviously ready to flee the spirit of death that encircled her heart.

Pulling cash out of her purse, the red head delivered the abortion fee at the payment desk. Services must be paid for in advance at this abortion firm.

The receptionist took the cash and handed the teen a clip board. As she sat down near me, I saw a tear fall from the corner of her eye.

As I watched, she carefully completed the requested information. I speculated that she listed a fake name like so many others in the room. Then I discounted that idea based on her seemingly pure presentation.

She only appeared innocent. She clearly was not since she was sitting alone in an abortion clinic.

When she completed the clipboard task, she stared at the other women in the room. Most were quietly weeping. Then she took a deep breath, closed her eyes, and put her head in her hands.

I could read her body language. There was a strange ambiance of holiness that seemed to encircle her. That Godly vibe did not fit in those surroundings.

"She's likely a church girl," I reasoned. "Afraid to be caught in a trap of sexual sin. She's such a hypocrite! Imagine if her mother knew where she was right now."

Suddenly the side door bolted open as an abortion clinic worker opened it. Dressed in medical scrubs, she called a strange sounding name.

The red head jerked as if suddenly awakened from a deep slumber. With obvious effort, she stood up and followed the attendant into the long, dark hallway that obviously led to the clinic's abortion theater.

My heart felt pity for the teen as I saw her shiver before the door closed behind her. If I had been in another place, I may have prayed for her. But this was no place for prayer. This was a place of death.

To occupy time, I thought about her circumstance. Her internal angst was nearly tangible.

Was she aborting to keep her parents from discovering she was no longer a virgin? Were there rules at her school that would have expelled her due to being pregnant and not married? Did she have a man forcing her to abort his baby? Did she want to make another choice?

Then a strange sound broke through the quiet office space. Horrified, I realized it was a woman screaming.

The noise seemed to be quickly muffled. Then it broke through whatever was attempting to contain it and the screams began again. On and off, I could hear that horrible sound.

"Must be the red head," I thought sadly.

While my heart wanted to free her from whatever was causing her such harm, it wasn't my place. I couldn't rescue her. She had made her choice and would suffer accordingly.

To escape the traumatizing sounds, I got up and walked out of the clinic. I then gazed into the parking lot outside which seemed quiet except for movement in one parked car. A young man was sitting in his vehicle, obviously listening to the radio.

"Must be her boyfriend," I reasoned with a grimace. "He is no hero. He waited in the car and made her come into the clinic alone! What a jerk!"

The younger man's appearance was clearly not as wholesome as the red head. As I was watching him, a sudden look of panic materialized on his face. His next expression bore the likelihood of an internal argument.

# Beyond Regret: Living Victoriously

I was quite shocked when he got out of the car and walked ten feet toward the clinic. His intense gaze appeared as if he was considering rescuing his damsel in distress.

Then he stopped and threw his hands in the air. His mouth was moving so I assumed he was talking to himself. When he turned around and headed back to the sanctuary of his vehicle, I knew he had talked himself out of liberating her.

He had changed his mind, I realized. He was no knight in shining armor.

When sufficient time had passed, I walked back into the clinic's waiting room and sat down again. When the door eventually opened, the red head was the first to emerge.

Our eyes met and **then our identities merged**.

I suddenly realized this red-headed teenage stranger was me. For eleven years I worked to assimilate myself into the personality of the teen who took the life of her own child that day. I was fearful of her possible return to do more damage to my life. I kept her well hidden in my heart.

While I certainly could blame others for encouraging my abortion choice, I had walked into that clinic out of my own free will. Therefore, I was ultimately responsible for my child's death. In going against my female "genetic code" to protect my "young" at all costs, there was a huge fine to pay in regret. A decade was a long time to carry that weight.

In discovering the common issues of post-abortive women back then, I realized that my pain was clearly related to my past abortion. As God lifted the curtains from my eyes regarding this past choice, Scripture outlined His grace, mercy, and forgiveness regarding ANY sin. My abortion seemed to not fit any biblical criteria, however. I felt like I was the worst of sinners, deserving any pain I encountered for sacrificing my child on the altar of "choice."

Spiritually sensitive post-abortive individuals often view their choice to abort as unforgivable in the eyes of God. Many also struggle in forgiving others who participated in their abortion choice. Post-abortive people are often the hardest on themselves for participating in their own child's death. Regardless of the sin, God does not hold our sins against us. He wants to forgive and heal our hearts.

Many post-abortive people pursue self-punishing behaviors like drugs and promiscuity because of the internal self-loathing that can result after abortion. It is easy to embrace a false belief that we deserve the worst in life for ending our child's time on Earth. Post-abortive people are often their own worst enemies.

During my own abortion recovery program, God used the parable of the Unmerciful Servant found in Matthew 18:21-35 to help me forgive myself. My abortion recovery leader asked me to view myself in two distinct ways:

As the richer servant whom the King forgave – *the current Sydna whom God had just forgiven the debt of abortion.*

As the second servant whom the richer servant would not forgive – *the 19-year-old Sydna who had chosen abortion.*

If God had forgiven my sin of abortion, He was requiring that I personally forgive the younger version of myself to realize His peace. It helped to know that younger Sydna no longer existed. Everything the former Sydna had been extinguished with each step of maturity God brought to my life. She was a separate person from the woman I was at that point.

The bitterness and anger I was holding against the younger version of myself had developed into a "bitter root" that prohibited any harmony in my life. Forgiveness was the only way to peace.

With a simple prayer, I asked God for help to forgive the woman I had been when I made that choice. Over several days, through Scripture, prayer, and encouragement from others, I was able to end the war in my heart and release myself from that prison of regret.

With the depth of this sin removed from my heart, God gave me a deep peace and a job to help other women considering abortion. It has been the biggest blessing of my life to help abortion's wounded hearts.

Since 1991, I believe I've spoken to more post-abortive individuals than anyone else on Earth, offering the same hope of God's healing. Second generations of families are enjoying life because God helped me share my abortion regret with mothers considering abortion. Being involved in ending abortion helped my heart as well!

I'm glad God is in the business of forgiving each of us, no matter what the sin!

## Comfort Scriptures

**Colossians 1:13-15** - *For he has rescued us from the dominion of darkness and brought us into the kingdom of the Son he loves, in whom we have redemption, the forgiveness of sins.*

## Activity

Take the time to place yourself in a position of someone observing you in the steps you took before aborting as I did on page 120 in the section entitled, "Stranger at the Abortion Clinic."

Outline what you looked like, acted, and endured in that time frame. Consider what those waiting for you might have been thinking/doing. It will help you gain more understanding about the younger version of yourself that allowed her child to be aborted so you can forgive her!

## Chapter 9 - Tackling Enduring Emotions

We must address our emotions of anger to begin the process of forgiveness. Begin by praying that God will direct you in how to address your angry feelings in the privacy of your own heart. Seek the root of the anger, bitterness, and pain to release it totally and completely.

### #MeToo and Abortion Pain

"My abortion was far more traumatic than the rape, Sydna," the young woman shared during an abortion recovery program I was leading. "Why didn't anyone tell me that abortion would be so hard? Even Christians recommended I abort but I didn't think it would be so brutal to my heart, soul and mind."

The #MeToo hashtag has identified many women who were abused in the past. Women who have experienced sexual abuse are often post-abortive as well. No matter what the reason for aborting, the physical, spiritual, and emotional encounter of walking into an abortion clinic and allowing a child to be removed from your womb is rarely an easy experience. When sexual abuse has occurred, abortion can ignite further devastation to these wounded hearts.

"My husband was beating me and had just started to hit my kids," the woman shared during a ministry call. "I aborted believing it was better that my unborn child never be born than to have such an abusive father. How could I have been so wrong?"

Abortion is often recommended in cases of abuse, rape, and incest. Even the staunchest pro-lifer struggles to discourage abortion should a woman enduring these circumstances become pregnant.

# Beyond Regret: Living Victoriously

Sadly, it doesn't matter what led you to have an abortion. *The pain on the other side of this choice can produce additional trauma at a physical, emotional, and psychological level.* During a time when these women need understanding and support, many feel pressured to abort by those who are attempting to "help" them.

Children who were conceived after such an abusive sexual encounter are now speaking out, highlighting their amazing lives despite living with the DNA of a criminal. They offer incredible stories of how amazing their lives have been despite having been conceived through a violent encounter.

"I remember my uncle taking me to a place where there were nurses, "a young woman shared with me. "I was 12 and it was a cold place where they made me get up on a table. I had no idea what was happening. It was terrifying and I begged them to let me go home. Then they put a needle in my arm, and I went to sleep. I know now in my heart that was an abortion clinic. I woke up feeling so empty. I was so sore down there that I knew something had happened."

Over the years I've heard the testimonies of hundreds of women who shared memories of early sexual abuse. Many recall their abuser taking them to a "clinic" but had no idea what happened to them there. They often outline they did not realize they were even pregnant. A sudden realization that they likely aborted children is an additional horror in processing their sexual abuse pain.

When abortion was made legal in the late 1960's in several states, sexual abuse rates were much lower than today. If a 12-year-old came up pregnant, society would search and prosecute the man who had abused her. *The pregnancy often revealed and then ended the sexual abuse.*

After the legalization of abortion, sexual abusers gained a tool that allowed them to dispose of the evidence of their rape and allow them to continue abusing victims. Pedophiles understand that the DNA of a child born from rape can lead to long prison sentences. Abortion removes the proof of their sexual abuse from existence, allowing them the horrifying ability to continue their abusive ways.

Many victims feel they have no other choice but to abort after sexual abuse. As discussed previously, many women walking through an abortion procedure live Isaiah 53:7 – *He was oppressed and He was afflicted, Yet He opened not His mouth; He was led as a lamb to the slaughter, And as a sheep before its shearers is silent, So He opened not His mouth.*

Sexual trafficking ministries have long understood the connection between abortion and sexual abuse. For those caught in the web of sexual slavery, abortion is a well-used financial tool for traffickers. Those that escape that sexual imprisonment often report multiple forced abortion experiences.

Internationally, the connection between sexual abuse and abortion is even more obvious. I once addressed a conference for women who were leading Central Asian sexual trafficking ministries. The previous year the event leaders had conducted a survey, asking if attendees had experienced abortion. Results from that study outlined the audience had a 100% post-abortion rate.

It was an honor to spend a week with many of these leaders, helping them find God's healing for their abortion pain. Ramah then provided the entire group with our abortion recovery resources and tools to take back to their nations to help the women they serve process their abortion pain.

Families that discover sexual abuse often refuse to support any resulting pregnancy. Even spouses can force a recently raped woman into an abortion clinic. If she wants to continue her marriage, she must sacrifice the child in her womb. When abortion leaves her even more wounded, no one knows how to help her heal. So, they ignore the topic, and the woman often wallows away for many years in shame and guilt.

Most rape kits offered to sexually assaulted women include the "morning after pill." This medication is designed to prevent pregnancy. Even taking this pill could cause further trauma as women have no idea if they lost a child. Many grieve despite never knowing if a child was conceived.

*Abortion is never a healing experience.* After sexual abuse, it can ensure an even deeper wounding. If someone you know has experienced sexual abuse, there is a good chance abortion was part of that trauma. It isn't wrong to ask them if abortion was part of their exploitation.

The healing process after abortion can be very similar to the path of restoration for a sexual abuse victim. Denial, anger, depression, forgiveness, and other stages of grief experienced by the post-abortive also are typical of the sexually abused woman.

The emotional trauma of keeping the secret of sexual abuse and/or abortion may manifest in self-destructive behaviors, inability to form or maintain personal relationships, or complete withdrawal from society.

Romans 5:5 reveals God's ability to heal the hearts of His people from any sin, even abortion. *Now hope does not disappoint, because the love of God has been poured out in our hearts by the Holy Spirit who was given to us.*

## Healing for Abortion's Ongoing Bloodguilt

"The man outside the abortion clinic called me a murderer," a post-abortive woman shared with me." He said that I would rot in Hell, Sydna. The blood of my little baby is on my hands. How can God ever forgive me?"

Bloodguilt results after murder or bloodshed. In abortion, the term fits.

When a woman exits an abortion clinic, one is dead and the other is often wounded. This mother also assumes a new title from society if they discover her abortion sin – murderer.

Post-abortive hearts often arrive at a false belief that in ending their tiny child's life, they have committed an *unforgivable sin.* Many then pursue other self-destructive behaviors, falsely believing they somehow deserve the worst treatment due to making this horrendous choice.

When we confess our sin of abortion, God forgives and heals our hearts and cleanses us from our iniquity. He can heal even the bloodguilt that marks an abortion experience.

Before we were born, God knew every sin we would commit. This truth is revealed in Psalm 139:15-16, *My frame was not hidden from you when I was made in the secret place, when I was woven together in the depths of the earth. Your eyes saw my unformed body; all the days ordained for me were written in your book before one of them came to be.*

As I exited the abortion clinic where my child had died, I distinctly remember realizing I had just committed the worst sin possible. The voice of the accuser – Satan – amplified that mindset.

In that angry and hopeless mode, I pursued other sinful behaviors which drew me farther away from God's loving voice. It would take seven years for God to pull away the clouds of sin that blinded me to His grace and mercy. That understanding arrived when I first stared into the eyes of my next-born child.

My healing experience included a direction from God to forgive everyone who impacted my child's death. One by one, I worked through the anger and grief as God helped me pardon each involved player. I was finally able to release them to God's divine judgment. The peace that resulted in my heart was phenomenal.

The next step in my healing was asking God for other names that I needed to forgive. When I heard a name in my heart, I balked. It made no sense that God would want me to forgive another murderer.

A year and a half before my abortion recovery class, my friend and neighbor was brutally murdered by a woman who was having an affair with her husband. It was Diane's death in 1990 that began my grieving process for my lost child.

When I heard the name of Diane's murderer in my heart – Jennifer Reali – I thought, ""She murdered a mother of three. She doesn't deserve forgiveness."

Instantly another message flew into my brain – "And you allowed your firstborn to die in an abortion clinic. Tell me how you are any different from Jennifer Reali?"

I knew that thought had not come from my own brain because I clearly would never have considered that perspective. Undeniable Godly conviction washed over my soul.

When God puts a task in your heart, it's best to surrender or He'll keep you up at night. After a long battle with sleeplessness, I hung my head and reached out to this murderer in prison.

# Beyond Regret: Living Victoriously

I wrote Jennifer Reali a letter and asked her to forgive me for hating her. This is what I felt God was leading me to do.

When I put the letter in the mailbox, I lost 40 emotional pounds. I expected nothing more from the correspondence but that initial peace.

I was shocked when Jennifer Reali wrote back. Her first sentence was, "Please forgive me for murdering your friend…"

My heart leaped when I read that sentence. I got down on my knees and cried. My bitterness shattered into a million pieces. Joy returned to my heart in that instant. *I realized God had pushed me to forgive Jennifer for my sake, not hers!*

I never realized what a gift it could be to my heart to receive this apology from such a notorious inmate residing in a state penitentiary. Jennifer accepted Jesus into her heart at the time of her arrest in September of 1990. Her apology sparked a friendship where she would bless me on many difficult ministry days with tangible encouraging letters.

Soon I discovered that before she had murdered my friend, Jennifer had chosen abortion twice. During our first physical meeting, she said, "I believe at least 80% of the women in this prison have chosen abortion. No one is ministering to our hearts. While we have many other sins that define our incarceration, no one in prison ever talks about their past abortion, even if they are convicted of murder like me."

We then reviewed the journey of three murderers from the Bible – Moses, David, and Paul. Jennifer ministered to my heart about the forgiveness God had given her for the bloodguilt of taking Diane's life. With God's help, she helped me release the bloodguilt from my heart at a much deeper level.

If God can take the murderous actions of three men that He clearly loved and used after they sinned, my bloodguilt of abortion could also be turned for His good. These biblical stories remind us that the fellowship of healed murderers can result in God's love flowing down into our World in a unique and powerful way!

Even in taking an innocent life, when we truly repent and ask God for forgiveness, it has been granted! This is outlined in Colossians 2:13-14: *When you were dead in your sins and in the uncircumcision of your flesh, God made you alive with Christ. He forgave us all our sins, having canceled the charge of our legal indebtedness, which stood against us and condemned us; he has taken it away, nailing it to the cross.*

Receiving the truth of God's forgiveness into our heart after abortion can be challenging in a world where divisive abortion politics are discussed daily in media outlets. We need to re-adjust our thoughts by embracing the truth of God's divine redemption daily.

Reading God's word daily is essential in this process. I'm grateful that God never wastes even our sinful past and uses everything to His glory!

## Addressing Abortion Clinic Verbal Abuse

"I can't go to that pregnancy center for abortion recovery. It's right next to the Right to Life offices and I'm scared of those people," the young caller outlined when I gave her a referral for an abortion recovery program in her area.

She went on to outline that when she was leaving the abortion clinic through a back door, she had been in great emotional, physical, and psychological pain. She shared, "I've never felt that low in all my life. I stumbled and nearly fell but a man waiting at the back door helped me to my feet. He seemed so kind, Sydna. As I got up, he said with a strange grin, 'I hope you are happy. Your dead baby will sit in that dumpster tonight while you sleep in your warm bed.'"

This memory launched her into a few minutes of tears. When she recovered, she continued, "How can I ever go somewhere where that type of person works? I had no idea I was aborting a real baby until that moment!" Clearly the protestor enhanced her wounding.

Many women share about encountering angry protestors in front of the clinics where their abortions were performed. This was the first time I had heard a story of a woman being abused at the back door of a clinic. Her story stayed with me as I worked to find her an alternate referral.

While there were no protesters in front of my Indianapolis abortion clinic in 1981, I could certainly imagine the horror she had experienced. Thankfully, I knew the local pregnancy center director personally. She took the time to meet with this wounded heart at an offsite location. With great compassion, this post-abortive person agreed to go through their abortion recovery program and now lives peacefully.

In sharing my abortion testimony, I typically avoid "right to life" or politically based audiences. I learned early on that being "pro-life" doesn't necessarily mean everyone loves God! I have only accepted a handful of such engagements, preferring to remain separate from anything politically based.

When I moved to Florida in 2000, I accepted one local speaking invitation from a pro-life group. I was lonely and hoping to make new friends in my community. After my presentation, the crowd disbursed quickly and without comment. Only one couple approached me.

The woman was crying when she spoke first, "Please forgive us. Please forgive us. We had no idea!"

Confused, I asked them what was on their hearts.

"We've yelled at women going into abortion clinics. We've used those terms – murder and kill – too many times believing we could shock the women into changing their minds. That rarely has worked, and your story outlined why," the husband responded sadly.

"On top of that, we've truly disliked post-abortive women. Sydna, we need to apologize but we can't find these women," the wife continued. "The only post-abortive person we know is you. We hope that in apologizing to you that you can share our regret with these women who have been verbally abused by clinic protestors. We have no other way to apologize except to never act the same way again…"

They were sincerely sorry, and I hugged them, knowing their hearts were full of repentance.

"I forgive you," I answered. "I'm one of the few individuals in the world that has the blessing of comforting these women. I'll share your apology with as many as I can."

The woman then said, "Thank you for opening your heart and sharing your testimony. We just didn't know and have a completely different perspective now. We will be kind and compassionate so you will always be proud of us!"

If you were verbally traumatized by abortion clinic protestors, please receive this humble apology from this couple into your heart. Remember some protestors are working for the clinic itself, knowing that such verbal abuse will drive women into the seemingly supportive arms of abortion advocates.

## Five Types of Anger After Abortion

Mark Twain said, "Anger is an acid that can do more harm to the vessel in which it is stored than to anything on which it is poured."

"I am always angry these days," the post-abortive woman outlined. "My mother forced me to abort. She took me to the clinic, waited outside and afterwards forced me to go shopping with her. She never once asked me how I was doing. I hate her, Sydna!"

Anger typically surrounds women before and after their abortion. Anger assists in addressing – or covering up – typical after abortion emotions like fear, guilt, longing, frustration, or hopelessness. Temporarily, anger can boost emotional energy allowing us to escape emotions of despair and desolation.

There are several types of after abortion anger:

**Scorned Outrage -** My boyfriend made my abortion decision, outlining he would support no other choice. He threatened me, saying, "If you make any other choice, I'll tell everyone it wasn't my child."

As I laid on that table, I had prayed he would heroically break through the door saying something like, "Marry me, Sydna. I want our child!" My hero never arrived to rescue me.

When I exited the abortion clinic, I was broken and in pain. I had been weeping moments before as I laid in the "recovery room." As I watched the father of my baby running towards me, the hatred began in my heart.

He picked me up and twirled me around. He then whispered in my ear, "Oh, Sydna, I thought they had killed you up there."

While I didn't say a word, I thought, "You thought they were killing me, *and you waited in the car?*"

I escaped his embrace, looked him in the eyes with contempt and my internal rage exploded. Our relationship from that point until we parted nine months later was blanketed with anger. We remained together only due to his threats. He was clear that if I left him, he would tell everyone at our small Christian college about my abortion.

Anger helped me eventually leave him. Anger gave me courage which propelled me to seek a better life for myself at a public university. That scorn led me into the arms of liberal pro-choice friends who all supported abortion on demand. *Anger after abortion can provide a sense of control.*

**Heartbreaking Annoyance -** After my abortion, I would often get angry when I thought of my lost child. Whenever tears would start to fall, I would literally stop and redirect the pain into anger.

One of the ways this worked was to place the blame on everyone else for my abortion decision. My boyfriend got the full gambit of guilt concerning my loss. Another source of angst was the Christian college I was attending. Had they not had the policy of expelling un-wed pregnant students, I may have made another choice!

As shared previously, I would often stew in negative resentment towards my mother for not being emotionally strong enough to handle my unexpected pregnancy.

Justifying our anger can put us in more control and can make us feel self-righteous and strong. But as anger flares up, it also depletes our energy, draining us and making us vulnerable to more painful underlying feelings.

**Internalized Wrath** - During the moments when I could not stop my tears with anger, I redirected my rage towards myself. Occasionally, I would have Godly conviction about my lost child. *How could I have done that?*

Whenever I saw someone that was the age my child would have been, I would flee the scene. Afterwards, I'd try to collect myself but sometimes I just had to cry.

Thoughts of my lost child were few and far between in the early days after my abortion. But as my life went forward, encounters with motherhood brought a new rage. Whenever I thought of my lost child, I'd feel responsibility at the core of my heart. *How could I adore the child in my arms without remembering my child lost through abortion?*

Self-punishing and destructive behaviors – like using drugs and alcohol to forget my guilt – were part of punishing myself for taking a life. They also helped me forget my pain, if only temporarily.

**Diverted Fury** - "I'm not him, Sydna" my husband said quietly one day. We had been arguing and a fierce fury came out of my heart towards him. He stopped the fight with that comment.

Tom went on, "Sometimes you act like I'm him – the one that deserted you and your child at an abortion clinic. I'm not him, Sydna, and I don't deserve to receive your misdirected rage."

I had not realized that all the pent-up fury that I had for my boyfriend was toppling out of my heart and impacting my family – particularly, my husband. That realization made me take every angry thought captive and start focusing again on forgiving the man that forced me to abort. Never again would my husband receive that undeserved rage.

**Righteous Indignation -** A very different anger emotion hit when God opened my heart to the truth about the abortion industry. *I began to research the commerce of abortion.*

When I learned that it was legal in the US to abort a child at any point, I could not sleep at all. Hating abortion doctors and workers was not Christ-like but it consumed me. The idea that they were still in business, wounding other women each day, was overwhelming.

Instead of hating abortion providers, God had me focus on rescuing those we could before they entered a clinic. He helped me tame that emotion and redirect it, allowing me a platform to communicate to post-abortive people. That led to talking to the abortion-vulnerable and rescuing many from making the same horrible choice.

Anger is an emotion that must be addressed in the recovery process. Anger itself is not a sin. It is how you deal with it that can be sinful.

Righteous indignation is something Jesus endured on earth when He chased the money makers out of the temple. But it can also cause you and your family harm if you do not control this hatred. Everyone, particularly in the abortion industry, needs God's grace. When you feel anger develop towards these abortion workers, ask God to help them exit the industry and find His healing.

## Comforting Scripture

**James 1:19-21** – *Everyone should be quick to listen, slow to speak and slow to become angry, because human anger does not produce the righteousness that God desires. Therefore, get rid of all moral filth and the evil that is so prevalent and humbly accept the word planted in you, which can save you.*

## Activity

As you think about your own abortion journey, consider the ways abortion changed you and how those changes impacted others. Record these thoughts and reflect on them with God in prayer.

## Chapter 10 – Thriving in Christ's Victory

Jesus died on the cross for ALL sin, including abortion. Do not let Satan's lies keep you bound any longer. Ask God to help you break free from those chains. You mustered up the courage to enter the abortion clinic that day; now summon that courage back again, this time to call on God.

**You are Not Alone!**

"There is no way that those abortion provider statistics are accurate," the pastor concluded as we discussed abortion statistics. "I've never heard anyone from my congregation confess to an abortion."

Just because women do not share their abortion stories does not mean we do not exist at every demographic level of our society. Most are sitting in silent prisons of pain, fearing the wrath of the world if anyone should discover that we allowed the tiny human inside our womb to die.

True and trusted information on the **American post-abortive demographic** does not exist at a statistically significant basis due to the following reasons:

**Changeable** – How you feel today may not be the same as how you feel tomorrow. Post-abortive people can be unpredictable and changeable. Additional abortions increase this impact as do other "life" events like the death of family member or loved one, infertility, subsequent pregnancies, etc.

Many are afraid to address abortion memories, fearing doing so could lead to a suicide decision. As a result, many spend great amounts of emotional energy over the years working to forget they ever made such a choice.

**Too Broad** – Post abortive people comprise a large section of all American women over EVERY possible demographic. How a poor woman feels about her abortion can be vastly different to the emotions of wealthy women. Women of faith may experience deeper levels of regret than secular women with no faith background.

**Rehearsed Innocence** — It is "typical" for post-abortive women to practice ways to remain tranquil when the abortion topic is discussed in their presence. Numbness or emotional distancing can assist post-abortive women in remaining calm when abortion is discussed in their presence. If they are rehearsing their silence, *they will likely never reveal their truthful feelings on a survey instrument.*

**Recovery Impact** — Some women initially cope well after abortion but later find themselves in great emotional upheaval over this choice. Others who immediately are overwhelmed with regret and grief can attend an abortion recovery program and go on to live in peace. Those who have found healing present vastly different survey information than those who may not be struggling anymore after abortion.

**Impact of Abortion Procedure** – Women who endure surgical abortions have vastly different experiences/emotions than those who utilize the medical (RU486) option. In addition, those who endured a late term abortion often go through an actual birth experience. Their pain and regret can be quite different as a result.

**Cultural Influence** – Since America is a nation of immigrants, it is a "melting pot" of cultures that have different perspectives on unexpected pregnancy and abortion. First-generation Americans are more impacted by an outside culture than those whose ancestors have lived here for many years.

Within some cultures/religions, the loss of virginity is a reason to expel or kill women, even if they have been raped. These women literally abort to avoid being publicly murdered. Within Christian cultures, where the sanctity of life is embraced, women abort to avoid bringing shame or judgment on their families.

**Research Methods** – Current research methods (standardized surveys) are typically inadequate in uncovering *deeply entrenched emotional reactions* for this "difficult to discuss" experience. Women are rarely truthful about their abortion on medical intake forms! If they are withholding information regarding their health, they likely won't be truthful on a generic survey form or with an interviewer who asks troubling questions.

**Which Symptom to Study?** – There is no agreement among researchers about which Abortion PTSD symptom (relief, depression, grieving, self-destructive behaviors, etc.) they should attempt to survey as it relates to abortion, nor what level of symptoms should be considered substantial.

**How Many Women Have Chosen Abortion?**

Ramah International typically uses Planned Parenthood's research arm – The Alan Guttmacher Institute – for most abortion references. I cite abortion provider's statistics simply because they are one of the few groups that come into direct contact with us.

When I founded Ramah International in **1997**, Planned Parenthood featured the following Guttmacher post-abortion statistic as part of their "Facts in Brief: Induced Abortion" research – *At current rates, **43%** of all American women will experience abortion at least once by the age of 45 years.*

# Beyond Regret: Living Victoriously

**In 2008**, through an updated version of the "Facts in Brief: Induced Abortion" research, Guttmacher adjusted the post-abortion rate down to *33% of all American women will experience abortion at least once by the age of 45 years.*

At the end of **2017**, this source reduced the number again, outlining that *24% of all American woman are post-abortive.*

Why has this post-abortion number changed so much over the years? The answer relates to declining abortion rates among other variables. I believe this has much to do with the impact of the pregnancy center movement which offers so many the real choice not to abort by providing support services.

The general post-abortion rate in the US must now be viewed across generational lines. *Older abortion rates must be adjusted for various demographic groups.* For examples:

At the time of my abortion, the post-abortion rate for my demographic age group was 43% of all American women. That leads to a basic conclusion that **the post-abortion rate for women over 50 would be 43%**. Think about it – *nearly half of American women aged 50 or older had at least one abortion.*

For women between **the ages of 35 and 50 years of age, their post-abortion rate is likely more in-line with the 33%** post-abortion rate.

For those under **35, likely their rate resembles the 24%** rate based on the 2017 Guttmacher statistical information.

Obviously, this is just my educated guess when extrapolating abortion statistics. *Due to my deep involvement in abortion recovery ministry over the last 30 years, I have likely heard more abortion stories than anyone else alive on Earth today.*

*My speculations are educated at a different level from those who rarely hear an abortion testimony.*

## God's Purpose in Abortion Pain

"I've confessed my sin, Sydna, to you and God," the woman outlined. "I've attended a weekend abortion recovery retreat as well. Why isn't the pain gone now? Why isn't God healing me faster?"

Post-abortive women often spend a lot of emotional energy in denying or forgetting their abortion ever happened. When the truth that a tiny human being was lost in the abortion process, emotional and spiritual pain can overwhelm our hearts, throwing us into long-denied grief. Painful thoughts about our past choices are hard to address because they hurt!

So why doesn't God just take away this pain when we come and confess our sin to Him? We all know that is within His power.

Whatever you may think, God doesn't enjoy watching His children suffer. *He has a reason for us to experience this pain if He requires that we endure it.* God will not waste our pain.

When God took the curtains off my eyes – showing me that I had lost a human being in choosing abortion – the initial revelation was overwhelming. I could not stop crying or thinking of this child in heaven. Sadly, it took eleven years for me to get to that point.

I then somehow expected that God would step in miraculously and sweep away all my emotional and psychological pain. He obviously forgave me, but He chose not to heal my heart instantly.

God knew about all the other sins that I committed after my abortion that had to be confessed as well. I had to work through each additional transgression with God's help after this class was completed. Because He created me, *God understood my heart could only bear so much at one time.*

As I waited for my abortion recovery class to begin, I thought of other fast ways to heal. Perhaps sharing my secret publicly could be a way to obtain quick healing?

Being the first woman to speak publicly about my abortion on a radio show that reached millions should have earned me some relief, right? Wrong.

Then I hoped that helping to save one child from abortion's fate could produce a deeper level of restoration from God. That didn't work either, even though a wonderful life was saved. I then ended up carrying a lot of other people's burdens long before I was equipped with God's deep healing to do so.

There were times when I wondered, "Was this agony a way for God to punish me for my abortion?" That idea didn't sit well in my soul because I knew God's character to be gentle, merciful, and forgiving.

Finally, I embraced that God's plan for my life must include experiencing this pain and working through it with His help. The ache wasn't His punishment but simply a consequence of my abortion choice.

Embracing the pain and the process of searching my soul through an abortion recovery program truly helped me heal. While it wasn't quick, it has endured and allowed me to do great things with God's help ever since.

# Beyond Regret: Living Victoriously

Over the years I have met a handful of women who truly did heal from this pain miraculously. In most cases, they did not know God at the time of their abortions. Their salvation experience included their abortion confession. I've never doubted anyone's healing. God clearly can do anything He wants to do. But this "instant healing" is rare after abortion.

Today I'm fully grateful that God loved me enough to know that the process of grieving was good for my heart. By withholding immediate healing, God's discipline was to let me face every angle of the pain of this choice.

God would also use this healing season to teach me love for others who had yet to be reached with the hope of His healing. Just as Jesus needed to come to earth to "walk in our shoes" as humans, I needed to walk through and understand my own pain before I could help anyone else.

In Psalm 94:12-15 David writes, *Blessed is the one you discipline, Lord, the one you teach from your law; you grant them relief from days of trouble, till a pit is dug for the wicked. For the Lord will not reject his people; he will never forsake his inheritance. Judgment will again be founded on righteousness, and all the upright in heart will follow it.*

If God simply removed the pain, we may not learn the intimate details of His love, mercy, and grace. This pain is something we need to understand to avoid sinning in the future, as outlined in Hebrews 12:7-11 - *Endure hardship as discipline; God is treating you as his children. For what children are not disciplined by their father? If you are not disciplined—and everyone undergoes discipline—then you are not legitimate, not true sons and daughters at all.*

Most have had human fathers who disciplined us, and we respected them for it. How much more should we submit to the Father of spirits and live! They disciplined us for a little while as they thought best; but God disciplines us for our good, in order that we may share in His holiness.

No discipline seems pleasant at the time, but painful. Later, however, it produces a harvest of righteousness and peace for those who have been **trained** by it.

Because I knew God when I made that choice, I walked away from His Holy Spirit's presence when I left that abortion clinic. I then believed that God had rejected me due to my abortion sin. Truth was, He didn't leave me – I left Him. Eleven years later, I longed to "partake" in His holiness once again.

The emotional and spiritual pain of the abortion healing process is a **temporary condition**. Tens of thousands of us have survived the truth of our choices, grieved our child(ren), allowed God's love to help us forgive those who harmed us (including ourselves) and come to the point of peace where God can use us in His kingdom. That healing is deep and changed each one of us in a good way!

Have hope that you won't feel this pain forever. Ask God to give you moments of peace to understand His love and discipline. He won't desert you ever and is always close to the broken hearted!

**I Never Heard From Them Again**

"I don't know how I'd ever have gotten through this without your help, Sydna," a ministry contact outlined in a letter I saved nearly twenty years ago. "You have been such a dear sister in this grieving process. What a wonderful release it has been to mourn, name and honor my child. I will always pray for your efforts, hoping many other women get the blessing of knowing you as I have!"

Ramah International's main goal is to help individuals experiencing abortion pain find God's healing. Whether this is by talking to them directly and helping them discover God's healing, writing blogs that answer their deepest questions, taking calls because they are pregnant again and considering abortion, or in referring them to local abortion recovery programs. We are always assured that God will somehow use us in their lives.

When someone sends me a message like this one, I typically never hear from them again. *Abortion pain, once processed, needs to be released.*

Our "identity" as post-abortive women need never be revealed to the world and this choice should never define us as an individual or as a mother. Any association or support of an abortion recovery ministry should always be led by God as well.

"Barbie" contacted us through our on-line healing website, HerChoicetoHeal.com, after one of my blogs hit a spot in her heart. We spent several weeks in direct communication before I comfortably referred her to a local abortion recovery program.

These efforts are a form of "triage," allowing the individual to prepare for face-to-face ministry services by processing their initial heartfelt concerns privately. Some never can be referred because no programs exist in their area. If that is the case, we continue to communicate until peace from God is achieved.

"Barbie's" abortion had occurred ten years earlier. She had been blocking (or denying) her abortion grief because she was terrified that if she touched that pain, she'd become suicidal.

A life event caught up with "Barbie's" heart in God's time. When her mother passed away, the grief consumed her. All she could think about was the child she had aborted who was in heaven with her mother.

God uses a wide variety of instruments to help us heal from our sinful choices. There comes a time for all His children to expose their secret sins to Him and reach forward, in repentance, for His grace.

God's healing is free. It comes with the mandate that Jesus offered to the woman caught in adultery. Jesus declared, *"Go now and leave your life of sin"* (John 8:11b).

"Barbie" was referred to a pregnancy center's abortion recovery program and I never heard from her again. After her child's memorial service, her class leader wrote to share how God had miraculously moved in her life. The harvest of God's healing in her heart changed her forever.

The only goal in abortion recovery is to help wounded hearts hear and understand God's voice in their heart. The revival in their soul does not necessarily mean that they are required to stand on a platform and share their story to help end abortion in our world. God often has other plans, whether that is another ministry effort or just in helping them be better mothers, sisters, daughters, and friends.

Some find that years later they need to talk again about their abortion pain. Elements of grief are often reignited during a lifetime. Local leaders come and go but most of these hearts remember their first point of touching this pain. It's my pleasure to help them navigate these additional emotions and set their hearts to understanding that God's healing isn't complete until we reach heaven!

Other healed hearts may write revealing they have discovered another friend who has experienced abortion. God's healing goes out – one soul at a time. A healed post-abortive woman is typically the only one who will ask the question, "Have you experienced an abortion?" Like a domino effect, coaching them in how to help this friend is a delight as it means God's healing is expanded!

John 4:34-38 shares a mandate for His people – *"My food,"* *said Jesus, "is to do the will of him who sent me and to finish* *his work. Don't you have a saying, 'It's still four months until* *harvest'? I tell you, open your eyes and look at the fields!* *They are ripe for harvest. Even now the one who reaps draws* *a wage and harvests a crop for eternal life, so that the sower* *and the reaper may be glad together. Thus the saying 'One* *sows and another reaps' is true. I sent you to reap what you* *have not worked for. Others have done the hard work, and* *you have reaped the benefits of their labor."*

If God has healed your heart from a past abortion, yet not led you to help others, **please pray for our efforts**. Pray for the millions that are still sitting in silent prisons of pain, waiting for God's release. Prayerfully consider supporting us financially with a tax-deductible donation if you are able. We promise it will be sown into fertile soil to return and bless your heart.

God is on the move and a great revival for post-abortive people is on the horizon. The harvest thus far that God has provided through Ramah International will soon explode exponentially. As a result of the last 30 years, these healed hearts now watch abortion politics and legislation efforts at a much deeper level and vote according. We need your prayers now more than ever before.

Wait… there's another message that has just arrived from our on-line healing website at HerChoicetoHeal.com. It's "Maggie" and her abortion was just three weeks ago. I gotta go and attend to her needs. It's harvest time!

## Comfort Scripture

**Jeremiah 29:11-12** - *For I know the plans I have for you," declares the Lord, "plans to prosper you and not to harm you, plans to give you hope and a future. Then you will call on me and come and pray to me, and I will listen to you.*

Made in the USA
Las Vegas, NV
30 April 2025

21552249R00085